Family Circle | **Cookies and Candies Cookbook**

Family Circle®

COOKIES
and CANDIES
COOKBOOK

FAMILY CIRCLE LIBRARY OF CREATIVE COOKING

A Practical Guide to creative cooking containing special material from Family Circle Magazine and the Family Circle Illustrated Library of Cooking

ROCKVILLE HOUSE PUBLISHERS
GARDEN CITY, NEW YORK 11530

on the cover:
Candies for everyone: (from the top, clockwise) **Almond Butter Crunch, Gum Drops, Easy No-Beat Fudge, Old-Fashioned Chocolate Fudge,** and **Creamy Penuche.**

on the back cover:
Sharp and sweet to the taste, **Peanut-Butter Crisscrosses** (top), and a collection of shaped and cookie cutouts (bottom).

opposite the title page:
A beautiful array of cookies and candies: (in jar, from top) **Lemon-Nutmeg Meltaway Cookies, Sugar-Crusted Chocolate Pretzels, Almond-Orange Confections, Coconut Gingeroons,** and (top, right, and clockwise) **Old-Fashioned Sponge Candy, Molasses Chips, Peanut Butter Fudge, Molasses Coconut Chews,** and on the tree, **Speculaas.**

Publishing Staff

Editor: MALCOLM E. ROBINSON
Design and Layout: MARGOT L. WOLF
Production Editor: DONALD D. WOLF

For Family Circle

Editorial Director: ARTHUR M. HETTICH
Editor Family Circle Books: MARIE T. WALSH
Assistant Editor: CERI E. HADDA

A QUICK METRIC TABLE FOR COOKS

Liquid Measures

1 liter	4¼ cups (1 quart + ¼ cup or 34 fluid ounces)	1 gallon	3.785 liters
1 demiliter (½ liter)	2⅛ cups (1 pint + ⅛ cups or 17 fluid ounces)	1 quart	0.946 liter
1 deciliter (1/10 liter)	A scant ½ cup or 3.4 fluid ounces	1 pint	0.473 liter
1 centiliter (1/100 liter)	Approximately 2 teaspoons or .34 fluid ounce	1 cup	0.237 liter or 237 milliliters
1 milliliter (1/1000 liter)	Approximately 1/5 teaspoon or .034 fluid ounce	1 tbsp.	Approximately 1.5 centiliters or 15 milliliters

Weights

1 kilogram	2.205 pounds	1 pound	0.454 kilogram or 453.6 grams
500 grams	1.103 pounds or about 17.5 ounces	½ pound	0.226 kilogram or 226.8 grams
100 grams	3.5 ounces	¼ pound	0.113 kilogram or 113.4 grams
10 grams	.35 ounce	1 ounce	28.35 grams
1 gram	0.035 ounce		

Linear Measures

1 meter	1.09 yards or 3.28 feet or 39.37 inches	1 yard	0.914 meter
1 decimeter (1/10 meter)	3.93 inches	1 foot	0.3048 meter or 3.048 decimeters or 30.48 centimeters
1 centimeter (1/100 meter)	0.39 inch	1 inch	2.54 centimeters or 25.4 millimeters
1 millimeter (1/1000 meter)	0.039 inch		

Contents

Straight from the heart—a valentine cookie easily made by you from **Honey Cookies** and **Sweet Sugar Frosting.**

Introduction

IF YOU THINK that cookies and candies belong in the repertoire of the professional cook, think again. Whipping up a batch of cookies and cooking a sheet of candies is not that difficult.

However, candy cooking is an art. Like yeast breads, they must be worked with the hands—kneaded, pulled, shaped, and decorated. And it is an art form in which the whole family can join.

Cookies, too, are fun to make. Whether they are drop cookies, named because they simply are dropped onto the baking sheet; shaped or molded cookies, that are shaped and rolled with the hands; press cookies which are forced through a cookie press or a pastry tube; rolled cookies; refrigerator cookies, which are first shaped, then chilled, and then baked; or the bar cookie, they provide both fun and creativity for the whole family.

To make your new family-art form easy, there are many tips dotted throughout this book. These give you the basic information about sugar and syrup, chocolate, or the many ways of working the cookie or candy into the required shape.

Look through your *Cookies and Candies Cookbook,* then set aside one evening for the whole family to join you in the kitchen. One evening is enough. After that, you'll have volunteers.

Cookie Jar Fill-Ups

There's lots of fun ahead of you when you make your own cookies. Whether cut outs, press, drop, pressed refrigerated shaped, bar or general shape cookies, you'll find many recipes that will set your mind to thinking and your hands to creating a multitude of fascinating cookies.

CUT-OUT FUN

Honey Cookies

The basic recipe for Valentine cookies

Bake at 350° for 10 minutes.
Makes about 6 to 8 five-inch cookies and
10 to 12 two- to four-inch cookies.

¾ cup honey
4 tablespoons (½ stick) butter or margarine
4½ cups sifted all-purpose flour
1 teaspoon baking soda
1 teaspoon ground cinnamon
½ teaspoon ground nutmeg
2 eggs
¾ cup sugar
½ cup ground or finely chopped almonds
⅓ cup finely chopped candied citron
1 tablespoon grated lemon rind
SIMPLE SUGAR GLAZE (recipe follows)
Red food coloring
SWEET SUGAR FROSTING (recipe follows)

1 Heat honey and butter or margarine in small saucepan just until mixture comes to boiling; cool to lukewarm.
2 Sift flour, baking soda, cinnamon and nutmeg onto wax paper.
3 Beat eggs until fluffy in large bowl; gradually beat in sugar; continue to beat until very light. Slowly stir in warm honey mixture. Stir in almonds, citron and lemon rind. Gradually stir in flour mixture to make a very stiff dough. Refrigerate, covered, overnight.
4 Roll out dough, one quarter at a time, on lightly floured surface to a ¼-inch thickness; cut into any of the shapes pictured. Place 1 inch apart on lightly greased cookie sheets.
5 Bake in moderate oven (350°) 10 minutes, or until light brown. Remove from cookie sheets

to wire racks; cool completely. Store in airtight container until ready to glaze and decorate.
6 Make SIMPLE SUGAR GLAZE. Divide into small bowls; color pink or red. Place cookies in a single layer on a rack, set over wax paper to catch drippings. Spoon glaze of your choice over each cookie to cover top and edges completely. To match our picture, set smaller cookies on top of larger ones before glaze dries. Let stand until glaze hardens, about 1 hour.
7 Make SWEET SUGAR FROSTING, then pipe through the writing tip of a cake decorator onto cookies in a curlicue design as pictured, or make your own design and special message. Let decorations dry completely, then wrap in clear plastic.

SIMPLE SUGAR GLAZE

2 cups 10X (confectioners') sugar
4 tablespoons milk
1 teaspoon vegetable shortening

Combine sugar and milk in a medium-size bowl; stir with a rubber spatula until smooth; stir in shortening until completely blended. Keep covered with damp paper towel to keep from drying.

SWEET SUGAR FROSTING

Makes enough frosting to decorate 6 large cookies and 12 small cookies

1 egg white
¼ teaspoon cream of tartar
1½ cups 10X (confectioners') sugar

Beat egg white and cream of tartar until foamy in a small bowl. Gradually beat in sugar; continue to beat until frosting stands in firm peaks and is stiff enough to hold a line when cut through with a knife. Keep frosting covered with damp paper toweling, to keep from drying.

Chocolate Valentine Hearts

A perfect way to say "I love you"

Makes 6 five-inch cookies.

6 *Honey cookies*
4 *semisweet chocolate squares*
  Red and green food coloring
  MARZIPAN *(recipe follows)*
  Candied violets (optional)

Melt chocolate in a small bowl over hot water; spread onto cookies to cover top and edges completely. Mix red food coloring in about one-fourth of MARZIPAN for roses and green coloring into remaining MARZIPAN for stems and leaves. Shape tiny roses, leaves and stems; press shapes into the moist chocolate glaze. Let stand until chocolate is firm, then write your message with SWEET SUGAR FROSTING tinted pink. The small chocolate hearts are decorated with candied violets and SWEET SUGAR FROSTING.

MARZIPAN

Makes enough for 6 five-inch cookies

Knead ¼ *of an eight-ounce can or package of almond paste with ¼ cup 10X (confectioners' powdered) and 1½ teaspoons light corn syrup in a small bowl.*

Tree Frosties

Easy to make and perfect on the tree

Bake at 350° for 10 minutes.
Makes about 4 dozen

1¼ *cups sifted all-purpose flour*
  ⅓ *cup granulated sugar*
  ¾ *cup (1½ sticks) butter or margarine*
  1 *egg, separated*
  1 *cup sifted 10X (confectioners' powdered) sugar*
  1 *package creamy white frosting mix*
    Green and red food coloring

1 Sift flour with granulated sugar into a medium-size bowl.
2 Cut in ½ cup of the butter or margarine with a pastry blender until mixture is crumbly; mix in egg yolk, then knead until mixture forms a stiff dough. Reserve egg white for frosting in

Step 4. Wrap dough in wax paper or transparent wrap; chill several hours, or until firm enough to roll. (Overnight is even better.)
3 Cut off one third of the dough; keep remainder chilled. Roll out to a 12½x6-inch rectangle, on a lightly floured pastry cloth or board; trim edges evenly. Cut in half lengthwise, then cut into triangles about 2½ inches wide with a pastry wheel or knife; leave cut-outs in place until frosted.
4 Mix egg white and 10X sugar until smooth in a small bowl; spread about a third in a thin layer over cut dough. Lift each triangle carefully with a wide spatula and place, 1 inch apart, on a greased large cookie sheet. Roll, cut, and frost each remaining third of dough the same way.
5 Bake in moderate oven (350°) 10 minutes, or until frosting is lightly golden. Remove from cookie sheets; cool completely on wire racks.
6 Prepare frosting mix for decorating with remaining ¼ cup of the butter or margarine and water, following label directions. Tint green and pink with food coloring. Decorate cookies as desired. Let stand until colored frosting is firm.

Lebkuchen

Heavily spiced cookie cut-outs that everyone in the family will enjoy

Bake at 350° for 10 minutes.
Makes about 5 dozen

  ¾ *cup honey*
  ¾ *cup firmly packed dark brown sugar*
  1 *egg*
  2 *teaspoons grated lemon rind*
  3 *tablespoons lemon juice*
3½ *cups sifted all-purpose flour*
  1 *teaspoon salt*
  1 *teaspoon ground cinnamon*
  1 *teaspoon ground nutmeg*
  ½ *teaspoon ground allspice*
  ½ *teaspoon ground ginger*
  ¼ *teaspoon ground cloves*
  ½ *teaspoon baking soda*
  1 *container (8 ounces) citron, finely chopped*
  1 *cup chopped unblanched almonds*
    SUGAR GLAZE *(recipe follows)*

1 Heat honey to boiling in a small saucepan; pour into a large bowl; cool about 30 minutes.
2 Stir in brown sugar, egg, lemon rind, and lemon juice, blending well.
3 Sift flour, salt, cinnamon, nutmeg, allspice, ginger, cloves, and baking soda onto wax paper.

4 Stir flour mixture into honey mixture a third at a time. Stir in citron and almonds. Dough will be stiff but sticky. Wrap in foil or transparent wrap; chill several hours, or until firm.

5 Roll out dough, ⅛ at a time, on lightly floured pastry cloth or board, to a 6x5-inch rectangle. Cut into 8 rectangles, 2½x1½. Place 1 inch apart on greased large cookie sheets.

6 Bake in moderate oven (350°) for ten minutes, or until firm. Remove to wire racks.

7 While cookies are hot, brush with hot SUGAR GLAZE, then press on a Christmas cut-out. Cool cookies completely before storing. Store in a tightly covered container at least 2 weeks to mellow.

SUGAR GLAZE

Combine 1½ cups granulated sugar and ¾ cup water in a medium-size saucepan. Bring to boiling; reduce heat; simmer 3 minutes. Remove from heat; stir in ½ cup sifted 10X (confectioners' powdered) sugar. Makes about 2 cups.

Christmas Cut-Out Cookies

With this one, you get two for the cooking of one

Bake at 350° for 8 minutes.
Makes about 4 dozen

4 cups sifted all-purpose flour
4 teaspoons baking powder
½ teaspoon salt
⅓ cup butter or margarine
⅓ cup firmly packed light brown sugar
⅔ cup light molasses
1 egg
1 teaspoon vanilla
ORNAMENTAL FROSTING *(see index for recipe page number)*

TEDDY BEAR COOKIES
(dark dough)

1 Sift flour, baking powder, and salt onto wax paper.

2 Beat butter or margarine with brown sugar until fluffy-light in a medium-size bowl; beat in molasses, egg, and vanilla.

3 Stir in flour mixture, a third at a time, blending well to make a stiff dough. Chill 1 hour, or until firm enough to roll.

4 Roll out dough, one quarter at a time, ⅛ inch thick on lightly floured pastry cloth or board; cut into Teddy Bear shapes with a floured cookie cutter. Place, 1 inch apart, on greased large cookie sheets.

5 Bake in moderate oven (350°) 8 minutes, or until firm. Remove from cookie sheets to wire racks; cool completely.

6 Make ORNAMENTAL FROSTING. Fit a small round tip onto a cake-decorating set; fill tube with frosting. Pipe decorations on cookies. Let stand until frosting is firm.

CHRISTMAS ORNAMENT COOKIES
(light dough)

Substitute ⅔ cup honey for the molasses and 1 teaspoon lemon extract for the vanilla in above recipe. Roll out dough; cut into Christmas ornament shapes with a floured cookie cutter, or make your own cardboard pattern, cutting out dough around pattern with a sharp knife. Bake and cool, following directions for TEDDY BEAR COOKIES. Brush tops of cookies lightly with corn syrup in a Christmas ornament design; then sprinkle with colored sugars. Let stand until designs are set.

Sugar Cookie Cut-Outs

You don't need a Piñata to enjoy Mexico at Christmas-time—just the Mexican Chocolate Horses

Bake at 350° for 10 minutes.
Makes about 5 dozen

3¼ cups sifted all-purpose flour
1 teaspoon baking powder
½ teaspoon salt
¾ cup (1½ sticks) butter or margarine
1 cup sugar
2 eggs
1 teaspoon vanilla
ORNAMENTAL FROSTING *(see index for recipe page number)*

BLUE BELLS

1 Sift flour, baking powder, and salt onto wax paper.

2 Beat butter or margarine with sugar until fluffy-light in a large bowl. Beat in eggs and vanilla. Stir in flour mixture, a third at a time, blending well to make a stiff dough. Chill several hours or overnight, until firm enough to roll.

3 Roll out dough, one quarter at a time, ⅛ inch thick, on a lightly floured pastry cloth or board; cut into bell shapes with a floured cookie cutter. Place, 1 inch apart, on large cookie sheets. Reroll and cut out all trimmings.

4 Bake in moderate oven (350°) 10 minutes,

(continued)

or until firm and lightly golden. Remove from cookie sheets to wire racks; cool completely.

5 Make ORNAMENTAL FROSTING. Tint ½ cup of the frosting a pale blue with a few drops of blue food coloring in a small bowl. Stir in 2 tablespoons water to make a thin glaze. Dip tops of cookies in glaze; turn right side up; let stand until set. Fit a small round tip onto a cake-decorating set. Fill tube with remaining frosting. Pipe a white outline and small bow on each glazed cookie.

MEXICAN CHOCOLATE HORSES

Prepare SUGAR COOKIE CUTOUT dough, adding 2 envelopes (1 ounce each) liquid unsweetened chocolate with the eggs and vanilla in Step 2. Roll out dough; cut into horse shapes with a floured 2½-inch cookie cutter. Place 1 inch apart on lightly greased large cookie sheets. Bake and cool, following BLUE BELLS' directions above. Make ORNAMENTAL FROSTING. Divide evenly into 4 small bowls. Tint deep pink, orange, and yellow with a few drops of food coloring. Fit tip onto a cake-decorating set. Fill tube with remaining white frosting. Pipe outline of white around horse. Pipe stripes of colored frosting on sides of horse to resemble a striped Mexican blanket, washing decorating set as you change colors. Let stand until frosting is firm.

Springerle

Small delicacies that go with any party

Preheat to 375°.
Bake at 300° for 15 minutes.
Makes about 6 dozen cookies

    4 eggs
    2 cups sugar
    1 teaspoon anise extract
4¼ cups sifted all-purpose flour
    1 teaspoon baking soda
      Anise seeds

1 Beat eggs in large bowl of electric mixer until very thick (this takes about 10 minutes); gradually add sugar, continuing to beat 15 minutes, or until very light and fluffy.
2 Beat in anise extract, then add flour and baking soda to make a stiff dough.
3 Roll out dough, one quarter at a time, on a lightly floured pastry cloth or board, to ½-inch thickness. Then, using springerle rolling pin, roll over dough only once, pressing designs into dough to a ¼-inch thickness. Cut cookies apart on dividing lines.

4 Grease large cookie sheets; sprinkle lightly with anise seeds. Carefully place cookies, 1 inch apart, on prepared cookie sheets. Let stand 24 hours, uncovered, in cool place (not refrigerator.) Cookies will appear to have white frosting.
5 Place cookies in moderate oven (375°) and immediately reduce heat to slow (300°). Bake 15 minutes, or until set but not browned.
6 Remove cookies to wire racks; cool completely. Store in tightly covered container about 2 weeks to season.

Molasses Midgets

These happy little fellows will charm the children! Cookies are thin, crisp, and rich with molasses

Bake at 350° for 6 minutes.
Makes about 6 dozen tiny cookies

1 cup sifted all-purpose flour
½ teaspoon pumpkin-pie spice
¼ teaspoon baking soda
   Dash of salt
2 tablespoons butter or margarine
2 tablespoons brown sugar
¼ cup molasses
   Currants

1 Measure flour, pumpkin-pie spice, soda, and salt into sifter.
2 Cream butter or margarine with brown sugar until fluffy in a medium-size bowl; beat in molasses.
3 Sift in flour mixture, a third at a time, blending well to make a stiff dough. Wrap in wax paper or transparent wrap; chill several hours, or until firm enough to roll. (Overnight is best.)
4 Roll out dough, ¼ at a time, ⅛ inch thick, on a lightly floured pastry cloth or board. Cut out with a floured small "gingerbread man" cutter or cut around your own cardboard pattern; place, 1 inch apart, on greased cookie sheets. Reroll and cut out all trimmings. Decorate with cut-up currants for eyes, mouth, and buttons.
5 Bake in moderate oven (350°) 6 minutes, or until firm. Remove from cookie sheets; cool completely on wire racks. Store in a tightly covered container.

Don't let the shapes fool you. These cut-outs, pressed, shaped, dropped and bar cookies are easy to make.

Merry Cut-Outs

Here's baking magic: Cut the same design in the center of each two cookies, then switch the centers

Bake at 350° for 10 minutes.
Makes about 7 dozen medium-size cookies

3½ cups sifted all-purpose flour
1 teaspoon baking powder
½ teaspoon salt
1 cup (2 sticks) butter or margarine
1½ cups sugar
2 eggs
1½ teaspoons vanilla
¼ teaspoon lemon extract
Yellow, green, and red food colorings
¼ teaspoon almond extract
Few drops peppermint extract
¼ teaspoon orange extract

1 Measure flour, baking powder, and salt into sifter.

2 Cream butter or margarine with sugar until fluffy-light in a large bowl; beat in eggs and vanilla.

3 Sift in flour mixture, a third at a time, blending well to make a stiff dough. Divide into quarters and place in separate bowls.

4 Stir lemon extract and a few drops yellow food coloring into dough in one bowl; stir almond extract and a few drops green food coloring into second bowl; stir peppermint extract and a few drops red food coloring into third bowl; stir orange extract into fourth.

5 Wrap each dough in wax paper or transparent wrap; chill several hours, or until firm enough to roll. (Overnight is best.)

6 Roll out half each of the yellow and green doughs, ⅛ inch thick, on a lightly floured pastry cloth or board; cut out each with a 2½-inch round or fluted cutter, then cut a fancy shape from center of each with a truffle cutter.

7 Place large cookies, 1 inch apart, on ungreased cookie sheets. Fit small yellow cut-outs in centers of green cookies and small

(continued)

green cut-outs in centers of yellow cookies. Repeat with remaining doughs.

8 Bake in moderate oven (350°) 10 minutes, or until firm. Remove from cookie sheets; cool on wire racks. Store in a tightly covered container.

Lemon Leaves

''Frosting'' of pistachio nuts, lemon rind, and sugar bakes right on these tiny delicacies

Bake at 350° for 6 to 7 minutes.
Makes about 25 dozen tiny cookies

2¼ cups sifted all-purpose flour
3 teaspoons baking powder
½ teaspoon salt
½ cup (1 stick) butter or margarine
1⅓ cups sugar
1 egg
1 tablespoon light cream or table cream
1 teaspoon lemon extract
2 egg yolks
1 teaspoon water
¼ cup finely chopped pistachio nuts
1½ teaspoons grated lemon rind

1 Measure flour, baking powder, and salt into sifter.
2 Cream butter or margarine and 1 cup sugar until fluffy in large bowl. (Save remaining ⅓ cup sugar for Step 5.) Beat in egg, cream, and lemon extract.
3 Sift in dry ingredients, a third at a time, blending well to make a soft dough. Chill several hours (overnight is best), or until firm enough to roll easily.
4 Roll out, a quarter at a time, very thin (1/16 inch), on a lightly floured pastry cloth or board. Cut into leaf or other fancy shape with a floured tiny cookie or truffle cutter. Place on greased cookie sheets.
5 Mix egg yolks with water in a cup; strain. Mix saved ⅓ cup sugar, pistachio nuts, and grated lemon rind in second cup. Brush cookies with egg-yolk mixture, then sprinkle with nut-lemon mixture.
6 Bake in moderate oven (350°) 6 to 7 minutes, or until firm but not brown. Remove carefully from cookie sheets; cool on wire racks. To store stack only a few layers. They're fragile!

Crown Jewels

Bright jelly filling twinkles atop each of these buttery gems

Bake at 400° for 8 minutes.
Makes 5 dozen

1½ cups sifted all-purpose flour
1½ teaspoons baking powder
½ teaspoon salt
4 tablespoons (½ stick) butter or margarine
¾ cup sugar
1 egg, separated
¼ teaspoon vanilla or brandy flavoring
2 tablespoons milk
¼ cup each mint, peach, and red-currant jelly
Silver candies

1 Measure flour, baking powder, and salt into sifter.
2 Cream butter or margarine and ½ cup sugar until fluffy in medium-size bowl; beat in egg yolk and vanilla or brandy flavoring. (Save remaining ¼ cup sugar and egg white for topping in Step 6.)
3 Sift in dry ingredients, a third at a time, adding alternately with milk; stir just until well-blended. Chill for several hours, or until firm enough to roll easily.
4 Roll out, a quarter at a time, to a ⅛-inch thickness on lightly floured pastry cloth or board. Cut into ovals or rounds with a floured 2-inch cutter, then cut a small oval or circle in middle of half the cookies and lift out with tip of knife. (Save to reroll and cut out along with trimmings.)
5 Place whole ovals or rounds on greased cookie sheets; spoon about ½ teaspoonful of mint, peach, or red-currant jelly in middle of each. Top, sandwich style, with a cutout oval or round; press edges together lightly with a fork or thumb to seal. Reroll trimmings, cut out, and fill.
6 Beat saved egg white slightly in a cup; brush over cookies. Sprinkle lightly with saved ¼ cup sugar; decorate with silver candies.
7 Bake in hot oven (400°) 8 minutes, or until golden. Cool on cookie sheets about 5 minutes, then remove carefully. Cool on wire racks. Stack not more than two layers high, with wax paper or transparent wrap between, on tray or in open pan.

Maybe the kitchen was a little hot, and there was flour all over the table. But when the end result is this collection of cookie cut-outs, it was worth it.

Chocolate Mushrooms

A round cutter and your fingers speed shaping. Recipe makes lots, but dough keeps well in the refrigerator to bake as you please

Bake at 350° for 8 minutes.
Makes about 20 dozen tiny cookies

2¼ cups sifted all-purpose flour
1½ teaspoons baking powder
½ teaspoon baking soda
¼ teaspoon salt
½ cup (1 stick) butter or margarine
1 cup granulated sugar
2 eggs
3 squares unsweetened chocolate, melted and cooled
½ teaspoon vanilla
5 drops red food coloring
2½ cups 10X (confectioners' powdered) sugar
5 tablespoons water
1 square semisweet chocolate, coarsely grated

1 Measure flour, baking powder, soda, and salt into sifter.
2 Cream butter or margarine with granulated sugar until fluffy in a large bowl; beat in eggs, melted chocolate, vanilla, and food coloring.
3 Sift in flour mixture, a third at a time, blending well to make a stiff dough. Wrap in wax paper or transparent wrap; chill several hours, or until firm enough to roll. (Overnight is best.)
4 Roll out dough, ⅛ at a time, ⅛ inch thick on a lightly floured pastry cloth or board. Cut out 1½-inch rounds with a floured cutter; lift away all trimmings. Then, with same cutter, cut an oval-shape piece from each round, leaving a section shaped like a mushroom cap.
5 Place oval cut-outs, 2 inches apart, on greased cookie sheets; shape each with fingers into a "mushroom stem." Lift caps and place, slightly overlapping, on stems; press gently to hold in place. Reroll and cut out all trimmings.
6 Bake in moderate oven (350°) 8 minutes, or just until firm. Remove from cookie sheets; cool completely on wire racks. Store in a tightly covered container until ready to frost.
7 Blend 10X sugar and water until smooth in a small bowl; drizzle over cookies; sprinkle with grated chocolate. Let stand on wire racks until frosting is firm.

Pinwheels

So rich they literally melt in your mouth! Whipped cream goes into the unusual pastrylike dough

Bake at 350° for 15 minutes.
Makes about 5 dozen tiny cookies

1 cup sifted all-purpose flour
½ teaspoon baking powder
6 tablespoons (¾ stick) butter or margarine
½ cup cream for whipping
⅔ cup strawberry jam (not preserves)

1 Sift flour and baking powder into a large bowl; cut in butter or margarine until mixture is crumbly.
2 Beat cream until stiff in a small bowl; stir into flour mixture, blending well to make a stiff dough. Wrap in wax paper or transparent wrap; chill several hours, or until firm enough to roll. (Overnight is best.)
3 Roll out dough, ¼ at a time, to an 8-inch square on a lightly floured pastry cloth or board; cut into 16 two-inch squares. Starting at each corner, cut diagonally through dough 1 inch in toward center.
4 Spoon a rounded ¼ teaspoonful jam in center of each square; moisten corners with water, then pick up every other corner point and fold to center, overlapping slightly; press lightly to seal. Place, 1 inch apart, on greased cookie sheets.
5 Bake in moderate oven (350°) 15 minutes, or until firm and lightly golden. Remove from cookie sheets; cool completely on wire racks. Store in a tightly covered container.

Taffy Twinkle Stars

They're like crispy shortbread with the rich flavor of old-fashioned molasses

Bake at 325° for 15 minutes.
Makes about 8 dozen

1 cup (2 sticks) butter or margarine
½ cup molasses
2 teaspoons vanilla
2 cups sifted all-purpose flour
1 cup unsifted 10X (confectioners' powdered) sugar
1 tablespoon water
Silver candies

1 Blend butter or margarine with molasses in medium-size bowl; stir in 1 teaspoon vanilla.

(Save remaining teaspoon for frosting in Step 4.) Gradually blend in flour. Chill overnight.

2 Roll out, a small amount at a time, to ¼-inch thickness on lightly floured pastry cloth or board. Cut out with floured star-shape cutters of varying sizes, or cut around your own cardboard patterns with a sharp knife. Place on ungreased cookie sheets.

3 Bake in slow oven (325°) 15 minutes, or until firm. Remove from cookie sheets; cool completely on wire racks.

4 Blend 10X sugar, water, and saved 1 teaspoon of vanilla until smooth in small bowl. Frost cookies; decorate centers with silver candies.

Holly Wreaths

Berries and leaves of colored frostings trim butter cookies

Bake at 350° for 10 minutes.
Makes about 4 dozen

1 cup (2 sticks) butter or margarine
1 cup granulated sugar
3 egg yolks
1½ teaspoons vanilla
2½ cups sifted all-purpose flour
    Green decorating sugar
    Red and green decorating frostings in pressurized cans or plastic tubes

1 Cream butter or margarine with granulated sugar until fluffy-light in a large bowl; beat in egg yolks and vanilla.

2 Stir in flour, a third at a time, blending well to make a stiff dough. Wrap in wax paper or transparent wrap and chill several hours, or until firm enough to roll. (Overnight is best.)

3 Roll out dough, one quarter at a time, ¼ inch thick on a lightly floured pastry cloth or board. Cut into circles with a lightly floured doughnut cutter. Or cut into rounds with a 2½-inch fluted cutter, then cut a 1-inch round from center of each. Place circles, ½ inch apart, on ungreased cookie sheets; sprinkle lightly with green decorating sugar. Reroll all trimmings and cut out.

4 Bake in moderate oven (350°) 10 minutes, or until firm. Remove carefully from cookie sheets to wire racks; cool completely. Decorate with holly berries and leaves, using frostings in pressurized cans or plastic tubes.

"Paintbox" Christmas Cookies

Cooking is just part of the fun—the family helps to paint the cookies

Bake at 350° for 10 minutes.
Makes 8 cookies

4 cups sifted all-purpose flour
2 teaspoons baking powder
1 teaspoon salt
¾ cups (1½ sticks) butter or margarine
1½ cups sugar
2 eggs
2 teaspoons vanilla
1 teaspoon lemon extract
        COOKIE "PAINT"
5 egg yolks
2 teaspoons water
    Food coloring

1 Sift the all-purpose flour, baking powder and salt onto wax paper.

2 Beat butter or margarine with sugar until fluffy light in a large bowl. Beat in eggs, vanilla and

(continued)

The newest way to decorate cookies is to "paint" cookies.

Roll out the dough to a thickness of ¼" between two sheets of wax paper.

With a small paintbrush, apply dark outline "paint" to the punched design.

Using the pictures in this section as a pattern, cut out with a sharp knife.

Fill in solid areas with appropriate "paint" to follow the pictures shown.

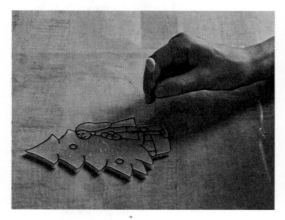

Punch holes through the pattern with a hatpin to outline the figure details.

Be sure to apply the "paint" thickly in order to prevent it from cracking.

Show off your skills as an artist—by
painting your cookies, following these
cookie cut-out patterns.

lemon extract. Stir in flour mixture, a third at a time, to make a stiff dough.

3 Beat egg yolks for "paint" with water in large bowl.

4 Divide egg-yolk mixture equally into five fruit-juice glasses. Add drops of different food coloring into each of four glasses. (The more you add, the deeper the color will be.) To make dark outline "paint," add blue, green and red food coloring into fifth glass.

5 Roll out a portion of cookie dough to a rectangle ¼-inch thick between two sheets of wax paper.

6 Cut out pictures shown on these pages for patterns. Place patterns on dough. Cut out shapes with sharp-pointed utility knife and trim away excess.

7 Punch holes through the pattern with a hat pin or needle along all the inside lines of figure details.

8 Lift off pattern.

9 With small artist's brush, apply dark outline "paint" to punched design.

10 Fill in all solid-colored areas as indicated on the patterns. Be sure to spread the paint thickly to prevent it from cracking during baking.

11 With a broad pancake turner, transfer cookies to lightly greased cookie sheets.

12 Repeat with remaining dough.

13 Bake in moderate oven (375°) for 10 minutes, or until firm and lightly golden in unpainted areas. Remove from cookie sheets to wire racks; cool completely.

Note: If you wish to hang the cookies on the tree, thread a needle with 8-inches of thread and run it through the cookie, at least 2-inches from the top. Tie ends to make hanger for attaching to tree. Shorter thread can be used if you wish to use a metal tree hanger.

Speculaas

These crisp, buttery spice cookies take marvelously to designing: press in blanched almonds or candied fruit before baking; when cooled, glaze or pipe on fanciful designs with decorator's icing

Bake at 350° for 12 minutes.
Makes about 7 dozen.

    4 cups sifted all-purpose flour
    3 teaspoons baking powder
    3 teaspoons ground cinnamon
 1½ teaspoons ground ginger
    1 teaspoon ground cardamom

    ½ teaspoon ground allspice
    ½ teaspoon ground anise seed (pound with hammer to grind)
    ¼ teaspoon salt
    1 cup (2 sticks) unsalted butter or margarine, softened
 1½ cups firmly packed dark brown sugar, lump-free
    1 egg

1 Sift flour, baking powder, cinnamon, ginger, cardamom, all-spice, anise and salt onto wax paper.

2 Combine butter (or margarine), sugar and egg in large bowl. Beat with electric mixer at high speed until light and fluffy. Beat in the dry ingredients slowly at low speed until mixture is smooth. Divide dough into 3 portions; wrap each in foil or plastic wrap and chill at least 2 hours.

3 Roll dough, one portion at a time, between two sheets of wax paper to a ⅛-inch thickness. Cut with fancy Christmas cutters or a 2½-inch round cutter. Place cookies on large greased cookie sheets. Press in any decorations you wish.

4 Bake in a moderate oven (350°) for 12 minutes or until cookies are slightly brown at the edges. Cool on wire racks. Store up to 4 weeks. Decorate with royal frosting, if you wish.

Pepparkakor

There's a lot of fussing, but you'll be rewarded with compliments

Bake at 350° for 7 minutes.
Makes about 8 dozen

 1⅔ cups sifted all-purpose flour
    ½ teaspoon baking soda
    ½ teaspoon salt
    ¾ teaspoon ground ginger
    ½ teaspoon ground cinnamon
    ¼ teaspoon ground cloves
    ¼ teaspoon ground cardamom
    6 tablespoons (¾ stick) butter or margarine
    ⅓ cup sugar
    ¼ cup light molasses
    1 teaspoon grated orange rind
    ¼ cup finely chopped toasted almonds
      ORNAMENTAL FROSTING (see index for recipe page number)

1 Sift flour, soda, salt, ginger, cinnamon, cloves, and cardamom on wax paper.

2 Cream butter or margarine with sugar until

fluffy-light in a large bowl; beat in molasses, orange rind, and almonds. Stir in flour mixture, a third at a time, blending well to make a stiff dough. Chill several hours, or overnight, until firm enough to roll.

3 Roll out dough, one third at a time, ⅛ inch thick, on a lightly floured pastry cloth or board; cut into fancy shapes with floured 2-inch cookie cutters. Place, 1 inch apart, on lightly greased large cookie sheets. Reroll and cut out all trimmings.

4 Bake in moderate oven (350°) 7 minutes, or until firm. Remove from cookie sheets to wire racks; cool completely.

5 Make ORNAMENTAL FROSTING. Fit a writing tip onto a cake-decorating set; fill with frosting. Press out onto cookies in designs of your choice; let stand until frosting is firm.

Cardamom Stars

These miniature cookies will charm all your guests

Bake at 375° for 7 minutes.
Makes about 13 dozen

2¾ cups sifted all-purpose flour
¾ teaspoon baking powder
½ teaspoon baking soda
½ teaspoon salt
½ teaspoon ground cardamom
½ cup (1 stick) butter or margarine
¾ cup firmly packed light brown sugar
1 egg
½ teaspoon vanilla
¼ cup dairy sour cream
   PINK GLAZE (recipe follows)
   ORNAMENTAL FROSTING (See index for recipe page number)

1 Sift flour, baking powder, soda, salt, and cardamom onto wax paper.

2 Cream butter or margarine with brown sugar until fluffy-light in a large bowl; beat in egg and vanilla. Stir in flour mixture, a third at a time, alternately with sour cream, blending well to make a stiff dough. Chill several hours, or overnight, until firm enough to roll.

3 Roll out dough, one quarter at a time, ⅛ inch thick, on a lightly floured pastry cloth or board; cut into star shapes with a floured 1½-inch cookie cutter. Place, 1 inch apart, on lightly greased large cookie sheets. Reroll and cut out all trimmings.

4 Bake in moderate oven (375°) 7 minutes, or

until firm and lightly browned. Remove from cookie sheets to wire racks; cool completely.

5 Make PINK GLAZE. Place cookies in a single layer on wire racks set over wax paper; spoon glaze over each to cover completely. (Scrape glaze that drips onto paper back into bowl and beat until smooth before using again.) Let cookies stand until glaze is firm.

6 Make ORNAMENTAL FROSTING. Fit a writing tip onto a cake-decorating set; fill with frosting. Press out onto cookies to resemble rays of stars.

PINK GLAZE

Sift 1 package (1 pound) 10X (confectioners' powdered) sugar into a medium-size bowl; beat in 6 tablespoons water until mixture is smooth. Tint pink with a few drops red food coloring. (If frosting stiffens as you work, beat in a little more water, a drop or two at a time, until thin enough to pour from a spoon.)

Medallions

One batch of dough makes enough for the base cookies, plus the fancy colored toppers

Bake at 375° for 10 to 15 minutes.
Makes 5 dozen double cookies

4¼ cups sifted all-purpose flour
¼ teaspoon salt
1½ cups (3 sticks) butter or margarine
1 cup sugar
1 egg
1 teaspoon vanilla
½ teaspoon almond extract
   Red and green food colorings
   ALMOND FROSTING (recipe follows)

1 Sift 4 cups of the flour and salt into a medium-size bowl. Set remaining ¼ cup flour aside for Step 3.

2 Cream butter or margarine with sugar until fluffy in a large bowl; beat in egg and vanilla. Stir in flour mixture, a third at a time, blending well to make a soft dough.

3 Divide dough in half; stir remaining ¼ cup flour into one half for making rounds for base; set aside for Step 5. Divide remaining half in two equal parts; place each in a small bowl.

4 Blend ¼ teaspoon of the almond extract and enough red food coloring into dough in one bowl to tint a delicate pink, and remaining ¼

(continued)

teaspoon almond extract and enough green food coloring into dough in second bowl to tint light green. Chill tinted doughs 30 minutes, or until slightly firm.

5 Roll out plain dough, ⅛ inch thick, on a lightly floured pastry cloth or board; cut into rounds with a floured 2½-inch plain or fluted cutter. Place, 1 inch apart, on ungreased cookie sheets.

6 Fit star plate or disk on cookie press; fill with pink dough; press out onto ungreased cookie sheets. Fit press with sunburst plate or disk; repeat with green dough.

7 Bake all in moderate oven (375°) 10 minutes for plain cookies, and 15 minutes for tinted ones, or until firm. Remove from cookie sheets; cool completely on wire racks.

8 Place about ¼ teaspoonful ALMOND FROSTING in the center of each plain cookie; top with a tinted one. Let stand until frosting sets.

ALMOND FROSTING

Mix ¾ cup 10X (confectioners' powdered) sugar with 2 teaspoons water, 1 teaspoon vanilla, and ¼ teaspoon almond extract until smooth in a small bowl. Makes about ½ cup.

PRESS YOUR OWN COOKIE

Spritz Cookies

This is a traditional Christmas cookie—so rich, so good

Bake at 400° about 10 minutes.
Makes about 12 dozen small cookies

2 cups (1 pound) butter or margarine (or use
  part shortening)
2 cups sugar
4 egg yolks
1 teaspoon vanilla
5 cups sifted all-purpose flour
  Nuts
  Candied cherries
  Tinted sugars
  Silver candies
  CREAMY FROSTING (recipe follows)
  Melted chocolate

1 Cream butter or margarine until soft in large bowl; gradually add sugar, creaming well after each addition until light and fluffy.

2 Add egg yolks, one at a time, beating well after each addition; stir in vanilla, then flour, a small amount at a time; mix well.

3 Pack dough into metal cookie press; press out dough into Christmas trees, bars, stars, and other fancy shapes onto ungreased cookie sheets; decorate some with halved nuts, candied cherries, tinted sugar, and/or silver candies; leave others plain, to frost after baking.

4 Bake in hot oven (400°) 10 minutes, or until edges are golden.

5 Remove from cookie sheets with spatula; cool on wire cake racks.

6 Frost plain tops with colored CREAMY FROSTING and decorate with tinted sugar and silver candies; dip ends of bar-shape cookies in melted chocolate.

CREAMY FROSTING

Beat 2 egg whites, ¼ teaspoon cream of tartar, and ¼ teaspoon vanilla until foamy in medium-size bowl; gradually beat in 2½ cups sifted 10X (confectioners' powdered) sugar until frosting stands in firm peaks. Divide among custard cups; leave one white and tint others with food colorings. (If frosting gets too firm to work with easily, stir in a drop or two of hot water.)

Spritz Slims

A tiny version of the traditional Christmas cookie

Bake at 375° for 8 minutes.
Makes 12 dozen

1½ cups (3 sticks) butter or margarine
 1 cup sugar
 3 egg yolks
 1 teaspoon vanilla
 ¼ teaspoon salt
3½ cups sifted all-purpose flour
 4 squares semi-sweet chocolate
 1 tablespoon vegetable shortening
 ⅔ cup chopped pistachio nuts

1 Beat butter or margarine with sugar until fluffy-light in a large bowl. Beat in egg yolks, vanilla, and salt. Stir in flour, a third at a time, blending well to make a soft dough.

(continued)

The man isn't traveling around the world in eight days. He's marveling at the many jewelled and glittering pressed—and bar—cookies in his balloon.

2 Fit rosette plate or star disk onto cookie press; fill press with dough (or fit pastry bag with a small star tip). Press dough out into 3-inch lengths on ungreased large cookie sheets.
3 Bake in moderate oven (375°) 8 minutes, or until firm; remove from cookie sheets to wire racks; cool completely.
4 Melt semisweet chocolate with shortening in top of double boiler; cool.
5 Dip ends of slims into melted chocolate, then into chopped nuts. Place on wire racks until decoration is firm.

To make CHOCOLATE SUNBURSTS: Prepare SPRITZ SLIMS dough, adding 4 squares melted and cooled unsweetened chocolate with the butter or margarine. Place dough in a cookie press fitted with a sunburst plate or disk; press out onto ungreased cookie sheets. Bake and cool as above. Decorate with frosting from a pressurized can, if you wish.

Almond-Butter Cookies

A traditional rich dough to squeeze through a cookie press into varied shapes; six are given here

Bake at 350° for 12 to 15 minutes.
Makes 7 to 8 dozen

    1 can (about 5 ounces) blanched almonds
    1 cup (2 sticks) butter or margarine
    ¾ cup sugar
    2 eggs
    1 teaspoon vanilla
    1 teaspoon almond extract
    2½ cups sifted all-purpose flour
    1 recipe ORNAMENTAL FROSTING (see index for
       recipe page number)

1 Put almonds through food chopper, using fine blade, or chop finely in an electric blender.
2 Cream butter or margarine with sugar until light in large bowl; beat in eggs, vanilla, and almond extract. Stir in ground almonds; gradually sift in flour, blending well, to make a soft dough.
3 Divide evenly into 6 small bowls. Flavor, shape, and decorate each variety, following recipes below.
4 Bake all cookies in moderate oven (350°) 12 to 15 minutes, or until firm. Remove from cookie sheets; cool completely on wire racks, then decorate.

Fit snowflake or star plate or disk on cookie press. Fill with dough from one bowl and press out on ungreased cookie sheets. Bake and cool, following directions for ALMOND-BUTTER COOKIES. Decorate centers with a swirl of plain ORNAMENTAL FROSTING; sprinkle tops lightly with dry cocoa.

CHRISTMAS CANES
Fit star plate or disk on cookie press. Fill with dough from second bowl and press out into 5-inch lengths on ungreased cookie sheets; turn one end to form a crook. Bake and cool, following directions for ALMOND-BUTTER COOKIES. Tint a small amount ORNAMENTAL FROSTING pale green with a few drops green food coloring. Decorate canes with frosting stripes; top with multicolor sprinkles.

BROWN-EYED SUSANS
Fit sunburst or star plate or disk on cookie press. Fill with dough from third bowl and press out on ungreased cookie sheets. Bake and cool, following directions for ALMOND-BUTTER COOKIES. Tint a small amount ORNAMENTAL FROSTING yellow with a few drops yellow food coloring. Decorate centers of cookies with a tiny swirl; top with semi-sweet-chocolate pieces.

PARTY WREATHS
Fit star plate or disk on cookie press. Fill with dough from fourth bowl and press out into 3-inch lengths on ungreased cookie sheets; join ends together to form a circle. Bake and cool, following directions for ALMOND-BUTTER COOKIES. Tint a small amount ORNAMENTAL FROSTING pale green with a few drops green food coloring. Decorate wreaths with a frosting swirl; sprinkle with red decorating sugar.

GREEN TREES and **HOLIDAY DAISIES**
Combine dough in remaining 2 bowls. Tint green with a few drops green food coloring. For GREEN TREES, fit tree plate or disk on cookie press. Fill with dough and press out on ungreased cookie sheets. Sprinkle with red decorating sugar; top each with a silver candy. For HOLIDAY DAISIES, fit sunburst or star plate or disk on cookie press. Fill with dough and press out on ungreased cookie sheets. Bake and cool both, following directions for ALMOND-BUTTER COOKIES. To decorate HOLIDAY DAISIES, tint a small amount ORNAMENTAL FROSTING pink with a few drops red food coloring; flavor, if you wish, with a drop or two of peppermint extract. Swirl in center of cookies.

Wreaths

Decorate these holiday treats with candied fruit

Bake at 350° for 12 minutes.
Makes 6 dozen

1 cup (2 sticks) butter or margarine
½ cup sugar
1 egg
1 teaspoon vanilla
2½ cups sifted all-purpose flour
1⅓ cups finely chopped walnuts
¼ cup maple syrup
Red and green candied cherries

1 Beat butter or margarine with sugar until fluffy-light in a large bowl. Beat in egg and vanilla. Stir in flour, a third at a time, blending well to make a soft dough.
2 Measure out ⅓ cup of the dough and mix with walnuts and maple syrup in a small bowl; reserve for cookie centers in Step 3.
3 Fit a pastry bag with a small star tip; fill bag with remaining dough. Press out into 1½-inch rings on ungreased large cookie sheets; fill center of each cookie with about a teaspoonful of nut mixture; decorate wreaths with slivers of red and green candied cherries.
4 Bake in moderate oven (350°) 12 minutes, or until lightly golden at edges. Remove carefully from cookie sheets to wire racks; cool completely.

Fruit Spritz

The secret ingredient is pineapple-orange juice

Bake at 375° for 10 minutes.
Makes about 10 dozen

4½ cups sifted all-purpose flour
1 teaspoon baking powder
Dash of salt
1½ cups (3 sticks) butter or margarine
1 cup sugar
1 egg
2 tablespoons thawed frozen concentrate for pineapple-orange juice
Silver decorating candies
Red and green decorating sugars

1 Sift flour, baking powder, and salt onto wax paper.
2 Cream butter or margarine with sugar until fluffy-light in a large bowl; beat in egg and pineapple-orange juice.
3 Stir in flour mixture, a quarter at a time, blending well to make a stiff dough.

Let friends share in your cookie excitement. Pack **Wreaths** or **Candy-Stripe Twists** into apothecary jars and deliver your seasonal gift in person.

4 Fit rosette, tree, or animal plate or disk onto cookie press; fill with dough. Press out, 1 inch apart, onto large ungreased cookie sheets. Decorate with silver candies or sprinkle with decorating sugars.
5 Bake in moderate oven (375°) 10 minutes, or until firm but not brown. Remove from cookie sheets to wire racks; cool completely.

Cherry Macaroon Puffs

Egg-white-light and chewy, with a tantalizing taste of almond

Bake at 300° for 20 minutes.
Makes about 4 dozen.

1 can (8 ounces) almond paste (not almond paste filling)
3 cups sifted 10X (confectioners' powdered) sugar
2 egg whites
1 teaspoon vanilla
   Red and green candied cherries, halved

1 Line 2 large cookie sheets with brown paper.
2 Blend almond paste and 10X sugar thoroughly in a large bowl; beat in unbeaten egg whites and vanilla until smooth.
3 Fit a star tip onto a pastry bag; spoon dough into bag. Press out into star shapes, 1 inch apart, on brown paper. (If you do not have a pastry bag, drop dough by teaspoonfuls onto paper-lined cookie sheets.) Press half a candied cherry on top of each.
4 Bake in slow oven (300°) 20 minutes, or until lightly golden. Cool on cookie sheets on wire racks; remove cookies carefully from brown paper with a spatula.

Meringue Stars and Kisses

Delicacies that are for eating—not decorating the tree

Bake at 250° for 30 minutes.
Makes about 5 dozen tiny cookies

2 egg whites
½ teaspoon cream of tartar
⅛ teaspoon salt
   Green food coloring
½ cup granulated sugar
   Green decorating sugar

1 Beat egg whites, cream of tartar, salt, and a few drops green food coloring until foamy-white and double in volume in a medium-size bowl.
2 Sprinkle in granulated sugar, 1 tablespoon at a time, beating all the time until sugar completely dissolves and meringue stands in firm peaks. Beating will take about 10 minutes in all with an electric beater. (If you prefer white cookies, omit food coloring.)
3 Attach a plain or star tip to a pastry bag;

spoon meringue into bag. Press out into kisses or stars, 1 inch apart, onto foil-covered large cookie sheets. Leave plain or sprinkle with green sugar.
4 Bake in very slow oven (250°) 30 minutes, or until firm but not brown. Remove carefully from foil to wire racks; cool completely.

Minted Meringue Trees

Peppermint dainties made with a pastry bag, decorated with candies

Bake at 225° for 1 hour and 15 minutes.
Makes about 3 dozen

2 egg whites
¼ teaspoon cream of tartar
⅛ teaspoon salt
½ cup sugar
¼ teaspoon peppermint extract
¼ teaspoon green food coloring
   Gold, silver, or colored decorating candies

1 Grease cookie sheets; dust lightly with flour.
2 Beat egg whites with cream of tartar and salt until foamy-white and double in volume in a medium-size bowl. Beat in sugar, 1 tablespoon at a time, beating all the time until sugar dissolves completely and meringue stands in firm peaks. Stir in peppermint extract and food coloring.
3 Fit a small star tip onto a pastry bag; spoon meringue into bag. Press out onto cookie sheets in tiny tree shapes, 1 inch apart, swirling meringue into a round at base and building up to a point. Sprinkle with decorating candies.
4 Bake in very slow oven (225°) 1 hour and 15 minutes, or until firm. (Meringues should not brown.) Cool 10 minutes on cookie sheets on wire racks; remove carefully to racks; cool completely.

Meringue Creams

Each little coffee-flavor shell is about as big as a half dollar and holds a billowy party-pink filling

Bake at 250° for 1 hour.
Makes 4 dozen

2 egg whites
1 teaspoon lemon juice
½ cup sugar (for meringue shells)
1 teaspoon vanilla

If it looks as though Christmas is the only season for cookie making, that's because there's more time to spend in the kitchen then. But make them any time of the year for a festive party table.

1 teaspoon instant coffee powder
1 cup cream for whipping
2 tablespoons sugar (for filling)
1 teaspoon brandy flavoring or extract
Red food coloring

1 Line two large cookie sheets with brown paper; draw 24 one-and-one-half-inch rounds, 2 inches apart, on each paper.
2 Beat egg whites with lemon juice until foamy-white and double in volume in a small bowl. Sprinkle in the ½ cup sugar, 1 tablespoon at a time, beating all the time until sugar completely dissolves and meringue stands in firm peaks; beat in vanilla and instant coffee.
3 Attach a fancy tip to a pastry bag; fill bag with meringue. Starting at center of each circle on paper, press out meringue to form tiny shells. (If you do not have a pastry bag, spread 1

tablespoonful meringue into each circle, building up edge slightly.)
4 Bake in very slow oven (250°) 1 hour, or until delicately golden. Cool on cookie sheets 5 minutes; loosen carefully from paper with a spatula; cool completely on wire racks. (If shells are made ahead, place in a single layer in a large shallow pan and store in a cool, dry place.)
5 About an hour before serving, beat cream with the 2 tablespoons sugar until stiff in a medium-size bowl; stir in brandy flavoring or extract and a few drops red food coloring to tint pink. Spoon about 2 teaspoonfuls into each meringue shell, swirling top to a peak; garnish with a Brazil-nut curl. Chill until serving time. (To make Brazil-nut curls: Cover shelled nuts with boiling water; let stand 5 minutes; drain. While nuts are still warm, shave lengthwise into thin strips with a vegetable parer.)

Whirling Stars

Set these on a metal dish—they look and taste heavenly

Bake at 400° for 10 to 12 minutes.
Makes about 5 dozen small cookies

1½ cups (3 sticks) butter or margarine
1 cup sugar
1 egg
1 teaspoon grated lemon rind
1 tablespoon lemon juice
4 cups sifted all-purpose flour
1 teaspoon baking powder
  Silver candies

1 Cream butter or margarine until soft in large bowl; gradually add sugar, creaming well after each addition, until mixture is fluffy.
2 Beat in egg, then lemon rind and juice; blend in flour sifted with baking powder to make a soft dough.
3 Fill metal cookie press with dough; press out into rosettes on ungreased cold cookie sheets; press a silver candy into center of each.
4 Bake in hot oven (400°) 10 to 12 minutes, or until edges are browned.
5 Remove from cookie sheets with spatula; cool on wire cake racks.

DROP COOKIES THAT WORK

Chocolate Crisps

You can count on these buttery drops, so rich with brown sugar and bits of chocolate, to disappear fast

Bake at 350° for 10 minutes.
Makes about 5 dozen

2¼ cups sifted all-purpose flour
1 teaspoon baking soda
1 teaspoon salt
½ cup (1 stick) butter or margarine
½ cup vegetable shortening
1 cup firmly packed brown sugar
½ cup granulated sugar
2 eggs

1 tablespoon rum flavoring or extract
1 package (12 ounces) semisweet-chocolate pieces

1 Measure flour, soda, and salt into a sifter.
2 Cream butter or margarine and shortening with brown and granulated sugars until fluffy in a large bowl; beat in eggs and rum flavoring or extract.
3 Sift in flour mixture, a third at a time, blending well to make a soft dough. Stir in semisweet-chocolate pieces. Drop by rounded teaspoonfuls, about 2 inches apart, on ungreased cookie sheets.
4 Bake in moderate oven (350°) 10 minutes, or until lightly golden. Remove from cookie sheets; cool completely on wire racks.

Butterscotch Crispies

Dainty wisps of goodness.

Bake at 325° for 5 to 8 minutes.
Makes about 10 dozen tiny cookies

1 egg
¼ cup granulated sugar
¼ cup brown sugar, firmly packed
2 tablespoons all-purpose flour
  Dash of salt
½ teaspoon vanilla
½ cup finely chopped walnuts
¼ cup finely chopped mixed candied fruits

1 Beat egg until light in small bowl; beat in sugars; stir in flour, salt, vanilla, walnuts, and fruits.
2 Drop batter in tiny mounds from tip of knife about 1½ inches apart on well-greased cookie sheets. (Mounds should be about the size of small grapes.)
3 Bake in slow oven (325°) 5 to 8 minutes, or until golden.
4 Remove from cookie sheets with spatula; cool on wire cake racks.

Ginger Jumbos

They'll remind you of big puffs of gingerbread—soft, light, and spicy. What a treat with milk, tea, or hot chocolate

Bake at 400° for 8 minutes.
Makes about 2 dozen

2¼ cups sifted all-purpose flour

Among the many types of cookies for young and old cooks alike, are shaped (left), bar (center), cut-outs (top), and drop cookies (top, bottom right).

2 teaspoons baking soda
1 teaspoon ground cinnamon
½ teaspoon ground ginger
¼ teaspoon salt
½ cup (1 stick) butter or margarine
⅓ cup sugar
⅔ cup molasses
1 egg
½ cup milk
1½ teaspoons vinegar
  Walnut halves

1 Measure flour, soda, cinnamon, ginger, and salt into sifter.
2 Cream butter or margarine with sugar until fluffy in large bowl; beat in molasses and egg. Combine milk and vinegar in 1-cup measure.
3 Sift dry ingredients, adding alternately with milk mixture, a third at a time, into molasses mixture, blending well after each to make a thick batter.
4 Drop by rounded tablespoonfuls, 2 inches apart, on greased cookie sheets; top each with a walnut half.
5 Bake in hot oven (400°) 8 minutes, or until

centers spring back when lightly pressed with fingertip. Remove from cookie sheets; cool completely on wire racks.

Sour Cream Softies

Cinnamon-sugar "frosts" the tops of these big, old-fashioned puffs

Bake at 400° for 12 minutes.
Makes about 3½ dozen

3 cups sifted all-purpose flour
1 teaspoon salt
½ teaspoon baking powder
½ teaspoon baking soda
½ cup (1 stick) butter or margarine
1½ cups sugar
2 eggs
1 teaspoon vanilla
1 cup (8-ounce carton) dairy sour cream
  Cinnamon-sugar

(continued)

1 Measure flour, salt, baking powder, and soda into a sifter.
2 Cream butter or margarine with sugar until well-blended in a large bowl; beat in eggs and vanilla. Sift in flour mixture, adding alternately with sour cream and blending well to make a thick batter.
3 Drop by rounded tablespoonfuls, 4 inches apart, on greased cookie sheets; spread into 2-inch rounds; sprinkle with cinnamon-sugar.
4 Bake in hot oven (400°) 12 minutes, or until lightly golden around edges. Remove from cookie sheets; cool completely on wire racks.

Oatmeal Crunchies

They're crisp and chewy with a good rich butterscotch flavor

Bake at 375° for 12 minutes.
Makes about 3½ dozen

1½ cups sifted all-purpose flour
½ teaspoon baking soda
½ teaspoon salt
  Dash of ground mace
 1 cup vegetable shortening
1¼ cups firmly packed brown sugar
 1 egg
¼ cup milk
1¾ cups quick-cooking rolled oats
 1 cup chopped walnuts

1 Measure flour, soda, salt, and mace into a sifter.
2 Cream shortening with brown sugar until fluffy in a large bowl; beat in egg and milk. Sift in flour mixture, blending well to make a thick batter; fold in rolled oats and walnuts.
3 Drop by teaspoonfuls, 3 inches apart, on greased cookie sheets.
4 Bake in moderate oven (375°) 12 minutes, or until lightly golden. Remove from cookie sheets; cool completely on wire racks.

Butterscotch-Oatmeal Crunchies

Bite into these spicy rich cookies and you'll find tiny pieces of butterscotch-flavor "candy."

Bake at 400° for 14 minutes.
Makes about 5 dozen

2½ cups sifted all-purpose flour
 1 teaspoon baking soda
 1 teaspoon salt

 1 teaspoon pumpkin-pie spice
 ½ teaspoon baking powder
 ¾ cup vegetable shortening
1½ cups sugar
 2 eggs
 1 teaspoon vanilla
 ½ cup water
 2 cups quick-cooking rolled oats
 1 package (about 6 ounces) butterscotch-flavor pieces

1 Measure flour, soda, salt, pumpkin-pie spice, and baking powder into a sifter.
2 Cream shortening with sugar until fluffy in a large bowl; beat in eggs and vanilla.
3 Sift in flour mixture, a third at a time, adding alternately with water, and blending well to make a soft dough. Stir in rolled oats and butterscotch-flavor pieces. Drop by rounded teaspoonfuls, about 2 inches apart, on ungreased cookie sheets.
4 Bake in hot oven (400°) 14 minutes, or until lightly golden. Remove from cookie sheets; cool completely on wire racks.

Cereal Crisps

Light and feathery, these disappear fast

Bake at 350° for 12 minutes.
Makes about 4½ dozen

1½ cups sifted all-purpose flour
 ½ teaspoon baking soda
 ½ teaspoon salt
1¾ cup (1½ sticks) butter or margarine
 1 cup granulated sugar
 ½ cup firmly packed brown sugar
 1 egg
 1 teaspoon vanilla
 1 cup oven-toasted rice cereal
 ½ cup quick-cooking rolled oats
 1 cup chopped pecans

1 Sift flour, soda, and salt onto wax paper.
2 Cream butter or margarine with granulated and brown sugars until fluffy in a large bowl; beat in egg and vanilla.
3 Stir in flour mixture until well-blended, then rice cereal, rolled oats, and pecans.
4 Drop by teaspoonfuls, 2 inches apart, on ungreased cookie sheets.
5 Bake in moderate oven (350°) 12 minutes, or until lightly golden. Remove from cookie sheets to wire racks; cool.

Brown-Edge Spicies

There's more than a hint of the Indies about these cookies

Bake at 350° about 12 minutes.
Makes about 3 dozen

2 cups sifted all-purpose flour
1 teaspoon baking powder
½ teaspoon baking soda
½ teaspoon salt
½ teaspoon ground cinnamon
½ teaspoon ground nutmeg
¼ teaspoon ground cloves
½ cup vegetable shortening
1 cup sugar
1 egg
1 teaspoon vanilla
1 cup canned applesauce

1 Measure flour, baking powder, baking soda, salt, cinnamon, nutmeg, and ground cloves into sifter; save for Step 4.
2 Cream shortening until soft in medium-size bowl; add sugar gradually, creaming after each addition until well-blended.
3 Stir in egg and vanilla; beat until mixture is light and fluffy.
4 Sift and add dry ingredients alternately with applesauce, blending well after each addition.
5 Drop batter by heaping teaspoonfuls onto lightly greased cookie sheets, keeping mounds 2 inches apart.
6 Bake in moderate oven (350°) about 12 minutes, or until cookies are lightly browned around edges.
7 Loosen at once from cookie sheet by running spatula under each cookie; cool on wire cake racks.
8 Store cookies in cookie jar or airtight container to keep them soft.

Brown-Edge Lemon Wafers

Smaller than snaps, but with just as much flavor

Bake at 375° about 10 minutes.
Makes about 5 dozen

¼ cup sugar (for topping)
   Grated rind of ½ lemon (for topping)
2 cups sifted all-purpose flour
2 teaspoons baking powder
½ teaspoon salt
½ cup vegetable shortening
1 cup sugar (for dough)

1 egg
   Grated rind of 1 lemon (for dough)
½ teaspoon vanilla
½ cup water
¼ cup lemon juice

1 Blend sugar and lemon rind (for topping) in cup; save for Step 6.
2 Measure flour, baking powder, and salt into sifter.
3 Cream shortening until soft in medium-size bowl; add sugar (for dough) gradually, creaming well.
4 Blend in egg, lemon rind (for dough), and vanilla; beat until mixture is light and fluffy.
5 Sift dry ingredients; add alternately with water and lemon juice, blending until smooth after each addition. (Dough will be very soft.)
6 Drop dough by teaspoonfuls 2 inches apart on greased cookie sheets; sprinkle tops lightly with lemon-sugar mixture.
7 Bake in moderate oven (375°) about 10 minutes, or until edges of cookies are light brown.
8 Run spatula under cookies to loosen from sheet; cool on wire racks.

Penny Wafers

A recipe your friends will ask for

Bake at 425° for 5 minutes.
Makes about 10 dozen tiny cookies

2 tablespoons currants
1 tablespoon hot water
2 teaspoons rum flavoring
4 tablespoons (½ stick) butter or margarine
¼ cup sugar
1 egg
⅓ cup sifted all-purpose flour

1 Combine currants, hot water, and rum flavoring in small bowl; let stand about 1 hour to blend flavors.
2 Cream butter or margarine until soft in medium-size bowl; blend in sugar, then egg, beating until light and fluffy; stir in flour and currant mixture.
3 Drop batter in tiny mounds from tip of knife about 1½ inches apart on well-greased cookie sheet. (Mounds should be about the size of small grapes.)
4 Bake in hot oven (425°) 5 minutes, or until edges are golden.
5 Remove from cookie sheet with spatula; cool on wire cake racks.

Taffy Rolls

Shattery bits of butter-nut goodness. They break easily, so pack carefully

Bake at 300° for 10 minutes.
Makes about 6 dozen

½ cup (1 stick) butter or margarine
1 cup firmly packed brown sugar
2 eggs
½ cup finely chopped pecans
¼ cup sifted all-purpose flour
½ teaspoon salt

1 Cream butter or margarine until soft in medium-size bowl; gradually add sugar, creaming well after each addition until light and fluffy.
2 Beat in eggs, one at a time, beating well after each addition; stir in nuts, flour, and salt.
3 Drop batter by small teaspoonfuls about 5 inches apart on lightly greased cookie sheet; spread thinly. Work with only 6 cookies at a time for easier handling.
4 Bake in slow oven (300°) 10 minutes, or until golden-brown.
5 Cool cookies on cookie sheet 3 minutes, or just until firm enough to hold their shape. (When hot from the oven they are too soft to handle.)
6 Loosen, one at a time, with spatula; quickly roll around handle of wooden spoon; place on wire cake rack to cool and crisp. While shaping, if cookies become too brittle, slide pan into oven for 30 seconds to soften them.
7 Bake and shape remaining cookies until all dough is used.

Parisiennes

They're rich-as-rich meringue cookies, each crowned with a chocolate topknot

Bake at 275° for 20 minutes.
Makes about 10 dozen

3 egg whites
1 tablespoon cider vinegar
½ teaspoon salt
1 cup sugar
4 squares, semisweet chocolate, grated
1 cup finely chopped almonds
1 cup (6-ounce package) semisweet-chocolate pieces
1 tablespoon vegetable shortening
¼ cup finely chopped pistachio nuts

1 Beat egg whites with vinegar and salt until foamy in large bowl. Beat in sugar, 1 tablespoon

at a time, until meringue stands in firm peaks. (This will take about 10 minutes.) *Gently* fold in grated chocolate, and almonds.
2 Drop by half-teaspoonfuls, 1 inch apart, on lightly greased cookie sheets.
3 Bake in very slow oven (275°) 20 minutes, or just until set. Remove carefully from cookie sheets; cool.
4 Melt semisweet-chocolate pieces with shortening in top of double boiler over hot water. Swirl on tops of cookies; sprinkle with nuts.

Currant Saucies

Applesauce, spice, and everything nice goes into these tiny thin drop cookies

Bake at 350° for 10 minutes.
Makes 10 dozen

1 cup sifted all-purpose flour
½ teaspoon baking powder
½ teaspoon pumpkin-pie spice
¼ teaspoon baking soda
¼ teaspoon salt
⅓ cup butter or margarine
½ cup sugar
1 egg
½ teaspoon vanilla
½ cup canned applesauce
3 tablespoons milk
¼ cup currants

1 Measure dry ingredients into sifter.
2 Cream butter or margarine with sugar until light in medium-size bowl; beat in egg and vanilla; stir in applesauce. Sift in dry ingredients, alternately with milk; stir in currants. (Batter will be thin.)
3 Drop by half-teaspoonfuls, about 2 inches apart, on greased cookie sheets.
4 Bake in moderate oven (350°) 10 minutes, or until lightly browned around edges. Remove from cookie sheets; cool completely on wire racks.

Tile Cookies

Let your children help before the cooking

Bake at 375° for 5 minutes.
Makes about 12 dozen

1⅓ cups sifted all-purpose flour

1 teaspoon baking powder
¼ teaspoon salt
4 tablespoons (½ stick) butter or margarine
¾ cup granulated sugar
2 eggs
1 teaspoon vanilla
2 tablespoons milk
Red decorating sugar

1 Sift flour, baking powder, and salt onto wax paper.
2 Cream butter or margarine with granulated sugar until fluffy-light in a medium-size bowl; beat in 1 of the eggs and vanilla. Stir in flour mixture, a third at a time, alternately with milk, blending well to make a soft dough.
3 Drop dough, ½ teaspoonful at a time, 2 inches apart, onto greased large cookie sheets; spread into 1½-inch rounds. Beat remaining egg well in a small bowl; brush lightly over each round; sprinkle with red sugar. (For easy handling, bake only 6 cookies at a time, for they must be shaped while hot.)
4 Bake in moderate oven (375°) 5 minutes, or just until lightly browned around edges. Carefully remove at once from cookie sheets and press each around the handle of a wooden spoon. Place on wire racks; cool completely. (If cookies become too brittle to shape easily, return cookie sheet to oven for 30 seconds to soften them.)

Fruit Cake Drops

So delicious, they are worth the calories

Bake at 350° for 12 minutes.
Makes about 12 dozen

1 cup sifted all-purpose flour
¼ teaspoon baking soda
¼ teaspoon salt
½ teaspoon ground cinnamon
4 tablespoons (½ stick) butter or margarine
½ cup sugar
1 egg
2 tablespoons brandy
1 package (8 ounces) pitted dates, chopped
1 container (4 ounces) mixed candied fruits, chopped
1 container (4 ounces) candied red cherries, chopped
1 container (4 ounces) candied pineapple, chopped
½ cup chopped blanched almonds
½ cup chopped Brazil nuts

1 Sift flour, soda, salt, and cinnamon onto wax paper.
2 Cream butter or margarine with sugar until fluffy-light in a medium-size bowl; beat in egg and brandy.
3 Stir in flour mixture, half at a time, blending well to make a soft dough. Stir in dates, candied fruits, almonds, and Brazil nuts.
4 Drop batter, a rounded teaspoonful at a time, 1 inch apart, onto lightly greased cookie sheets.
5 Bake in moderate oven (350°) 12 minutes, or until firm and lightly browned. Remove from cookie sheets to wire racks; cool completely.

Toasty Macaroons

Box these up and mail to a friend

Bake at 325° for 15 minutes.
Makes about 3 dozen

2 cans (4½ ounces each) toasted sweetened coconut
⅔ cup sweetened condensed milk (from a 14-ounce can)
1 teaspoon rum extract
¼ teaspoon ground ginger
Red and green candied cherries, sliced

1 Combine coconut, sweetened condensed milk, rum extract, and ginger in a medium-size bowl. Stir mixture until well-blended.
2 Drop by teaspoonfuls onto foil-lined large cookie sheet. Garnish each cookie with a slice of candied cherry.
3 Bake in slow oven (325°) 15 minutes, or until macaroons are firm. Remove from cookie sheet to wire racks. Cool completely.

Chocolate Meringues

Miniature meringues, they are so good to taste, you'll want even more

Bake at 275° for 25 minutes.
Makes 6 dozen

3 egg whites
½ teaspoon salt
⅛ teaspoon cream of tartar
1 cup sugar
1 cup very finely chopped blanched almonds
4 squares (4 ounces) unsweetened chocolate, grated
1 can milk chocolate creamy-type frosting
Green candied cherries, slivered

(continued)

1 Beat egg whites with salt and cream of tartar until foamy-white and double in volume in a large bowl. Sprinkle in sugar, 1 tablespoon at a time, beating all the time, until sugar completely dissolves and meringue stands in firm peaks. Gently fold in almonds and chocolate.
2 Drop by teaspoonfuls, one inch apart, on lightly greased large cookie sheets (or press through pastry bag fitted with a large plain tip).
3 Bake in very slow oven (275°) 25 minutes, or until firmly set. Remove carefully from cookie sheets to wire racks; cool completely.
4 Decorate each meringue with a swirl of frosting and a sliver of green cherry.

Lacy Molasses Rollups

They're almost like candy, and though they take a little time, they're so worth it!

Bake at 325° for 10 minutes.
Makes about 4 dozen

¾ cup sugar
½ cup molasses
⅓ cup water
¾ cup (1½ sticks) butter or margarine
1¼ cups sifted all-purpose flour
1½ teaspoons baking powder
½ teaspoon salt
¼ teaspoon cinnamon
1 cup finely *chopped walnuts*

1 Combine sugar, molasses, water, and butter or margarine in large saucepan. Heat slowly, stirring constantly, just to boiling; cool slightly.
2 Sift flour, baking powder, salt, and cinnamon into small bowl; stir in walnuts to coat well. (Be sure walnuts have been chopped finely or cookies will crack when rolled.) Stir into molasses mixture just until blended. (Mixture will be very thin.)
3 Drop by scant tablespoonfuls, 3 inches apart, on greased cookie sheets. (Make only 6 cookies at a time for easy handling. To save time, use two cookie sheets and bake one batch while shaping the other.)
4 Bake in slow oven (325°) 10 minutes, or until a rich dark brown. Cool on cookie sheet 1 minute, or just until firm enough to handle.
5 Loosen with spatula but do not remove from cookie sheet. Quickly roll into a cylinder with fingers; place, seam side down, on wire racks to cool and crisp. (If cookies become too brittle to shape easily, return cookie sheet to oven for 30 seconds to soften them.) These dainties do not store well. Enjoy them!

Chocolate-Pecan Rounds

Wheat germ adds a nutlike extra flavor to these crisp sweet treats

Bake at 350° for 10 minutes.
Makes about 5 dozen

1½ cups sifted all-purpose flour
½ teaspoon baking soda
¼ teaspoon salt
½ cup regular wheat germ
1 cup coarsely chopped pecans
2 squares unsweetened chocolate
½ cup (1 stick) butter or margarine
½ cup granulated sugar
½ cup firmly packed light brown sugar
1 egg
⅓ cup milk
2 teaspoons vanilla

1 Sift flour, soda, and salt into a medium-size bowl; stir in wheat germ and pecans.
2 Melt chocolate with butter or margarine in the top of a double boiler over simmering water; pour into a large bowl. Cool to lukewarm.
3 Beat granulated and brown sugars into chocolate mixture; beat in egg, milk, and vanilla. Stir in flour mixture until well-blended. Drop by rounded teaspoonsful onto lightly greased cookie sheets.
4 Bake in moderate oven (350°) 10 minutes, or until firm. Remove from cookie sheets to wire racks; cool completely.

Banana-Date Puffs

Soft, moist, and spicy. They'll remind you somewhat of little cakes

Bake at 375° for 10 minutes.
Makes about 5 dozen

3 cups sifted all-purpose flour
1 teaspoon baking soda
1 teaspoon pumpkin-pie spice
½ teaspoon salt
¾ cup (1½ sticks) butter or margarine
¾ cup firmly packed light brown sugar
1 egg
2 medium-size ripe bananas, mashed (1 cup)
1 teaspoon vanilla
1 cup chopped dates

1 Sift flour, soda, pumpkin-pie spice, and salt onto wax paper.
2 Cream butter or margarine with brown sugar

(continued)

Three favorites that are good to taste and are excellent as gifts, **Lacy Molasses Rollups, Shortbread,** and gumdrop- or chocolate-trimmed **Swedish Candy Nuggets** (see index).

until fluffy-light in a large bowl; beat in egg, mashed bananas, and vanilla. Stir in flour mixture, half at a time, until well-blended; stir in dates. Drop by rounded teaspoonsful onto lightly greased cookie sheets.

3 Bake in moderate oven (375°) 10 minutes, or until firm and lightly golden around edges. Remove from cookie sheets to wire racks; cool completely.

Toll House Cookies

These are popular give-aways during the end-of-year festivities

Bake at 375° for 10 to 12 minutes.
Makes about 4 dozen cookies

1 cup plus 2 tablespoons sifted all-purpose flour
½ teaspoon baking soda
¼ teaspoon salt
½ cup butter or margarine
⅓ cup plus 1 tablespoon granulated sugar
⅓ cup plus 1 tablespoon firmly packed light brown sugar
1 teaspoon vanilla
1 egg

1 package (6 ounces) semisweet-chocolate pieces
⅔ cup chopped pecans

1 Sift flour, baking soda and salt onto a piece of wax paper.
2 Cream butter or margarine, sugars and vanilla until light and fluffy. Beat in egg.
3 Mix in dry ingredients; stir in chocolate pieces and pecans.
4 Drop onto lightly greased cookie sheets, spacing cookies about 2 inches apart. Bake 10 to 12 minutes until lightly browned around the edges. Transfer to wire racks to cool. Store in an airtight cannister.

Cherry-Coconut Chews

For lunch boxes, teatime, or dessert with fruit or sherbet, they're winners!

Bake at 375° for 10 minutes.
Makes about 4½ dozen

2 cups sifted all-purpose flour
½ teaspoon baking powder
½ teaspoon baking soda
½ teaspoon salt

When the family calls out for more cookies, try the classic **Toll House Cookies.** Nobody will be disappointed.

⅔ cup vegetable shortening
⅔ cup sugar
1 egg
½ cup milk
1 teaspoon vanilla
1 cup flaked coconut
¼ cup chopped maraschino cherries, drained

1 Sift flour, baking powder, soda, and salt onto wax paper.
2 Cream shortening with sugar until fluffy-light in a large bowl; beat in egg, milk, and vanilla. Stir in flour mixture until well-blended; stir in coconut and cherries. Drop by rounded teaspoonful onto lightly greased cookie sheets.
3 Bake in moderate oven (375°) 10 minutes, or until firm and lightly golden around edges. Remove from cookie sheets to wire racks; cool completely.

Sesame Lace Wafers

More candy than cookie, these crispies are fragile and call for careful handling

Bake at 325° for 10 minutes.
Makes about 12 dozen

½ cup sifted all-purpose flour
½ teaspoon baking powder
  Dash of salt
¼ cup granulated sugar
¼ cup dark corn syrup
4 tablespoons (½ stick) butter or margarine
1 tablespoon water
¼ cup sesame seeds
  Colored decorating sugar

1 Measure flour, baking powder, and salt into a sifter.
2 Combine granulated sugar, corn syrup, butter or margarine, and water in a small saucepan. Heat, stirring constantly, to boiling, then cook, stirring often, 5 minutes; remove from heat. Cool 5 minutes.
3 Sift flour mixture over syrup in pan, then stir in; stir in sesame seeds.
4 Drop by ¼ teaspoonfuls, 3 inches apart, onto greased cookie sheets. (Dough will spread, bubble, and become lacelike as it bakes.)
5 Bake in slow oven (325°) 10 minutes, or until brown. Sprinkle with colored sugar. Let stand on cookie sheets on wire racks 1 minute to firm, then remove carefully to racks; cool completely.

REFRIGERATOR COOKIE SPECIALS

Slice-a-Fancy-Cookies

This is the basic cookie—below are three recipes using the dough

Bake at 350° for 10 minutes.
Makes about 12 dozen

4 cups sifted all-purpose flour
1 teaspoon baking powder
1 teaspoon salt
¼ teaspoon baking soda
1¼ cups (2½ sticks) butter or margarine
1 cup firmly packed light brown sugar
½ cup granulated sugar
2 eggs
2 teaspoons vanilla

1 Sift flour, baking powder, salt, and baking soda onto wax paper.
2 Beat butter or margarine with brown and granulated sugars until fluffy-light in a large bowl; beat in eggs and vanilla. Stir in flour mixture, a third at a time, blending well to make a soft dough.
3 Divide evenly into 3 bowls. Flavor, shape, and decorate each variety, following recipes below.
4 Bake all cookies in moderate oven (350°) 10 minutes, or until golden. Remove from cookie sheets to wire racks; cool completely.

RIBBON FANCIES

Divide one bowl of dough in half. Tint one half green with a few drops of green food coloring; leave other half plain. Roll out each half to a 9x3-inch rectangle between sheets of wax paper; chill in freezer 10 minutes; halve each rectangle lengthwise, cutting through wax paper; peel off top sheets. Brush tops very lightly with milk. Lay one plain strip, paper side up, on top of green strip and peel off paper; repeat with remaining strips, alternating colors, to make 4 layers. Wrap in wax paper or foil; chill several hours, or freeze, until very firm. When ready to bake, unwrap dough and slice into ⅛ inch-thick rectangles with a sharp knife; place on greased large cookie sheets. Bake and cool, following directions for SLICE-A-FANCY COOKIES.

PINWHEEL TWIRLS

Divide second bowl of dough in half. Tint one half deep pink with a few drops of red food
(continued)

coloring; leave other half plain. Roll out each half to a 9x9-inch square between sheets of wax paper; peel off top sheets. Lay pink-tinted dough, paper side up, on top of plain dough; peel off paper. Roll up doughs tightly, jelly-roll fashion. Wrap in wax paper or foil; chill until very firm. When ready to bake, unwrap dough and slice into ⅛ inch-thick rounds with a sharp knife; place on greased large cookie sheets. Bake and cool, following directions for SLICE-A-FANCY COOKIES.

CHECKERBOARDS

Divide third bowl of dough in half. Blend ½ square unsweetened chocolate, melted and cooled, into one half; leave other half plain. Roll out each half to a 9x3-inch rectangle between sheets of wax paper; chill. Peel off top sheets. Cut each rectangle lengthwise into 8 strips, each ⅜ inch wide. Carefully lift a chocolate strip with a long-blade spatula and place on a clean sheet of wax paper or foil; lay a plain strip close to it, then repeat with a chocolate and plain strip to make a four-stripe ribbon, about 1½ inches wide. Brush very lightly with milk. Build a second, third, and fourth layer, alternating plain and chocolate strips each time and brushing each layer with milk before adding the next one. Wrap in wax paper or foil; chill. When ready to bake, unwrap dough and slice ⅛ inch-thick rectangles with a sharp knife; place on greased large cookie sheets. Bake and cool, following directions for SLICE-A-FANCY COOKIES.

Strawberry Jim-Jams

Jam-and-walnut filling twirls inside these buttery pinwheels.

Bake at 375° for 10 minutes.
Makes 4 dozen

 2 cups sifted all-purpose flour
½ teaspoon baking powder
½ teaspoon ground nutmeg
¼ teaspoon salt
½ cup (1 stick) butter or margarine
½ cup granulated sugar
¼ cup firmly packed brown sugar
 1 egg
 1 teaspoon vanilla
½ cup finely chopped walnuts (from a 4-ounce can)
½ cup strawberry jam (from a 12-ounce jar)

1 Sift regular flour, baking powder, nutmeg, and salt into a small bowl.
2 Cream butter or margarine with granulated and brown sugars until fluffy in a large bowl; beat in egg and vanilla.
3 Stir in flour mixture, half at a time, blending well to make a stiff dough. Chill dough several hours, or until it is firm enough to roll. (Overnight is even better.)
4 Roll out dough to a rectangle, 15x12, on a lightly floured pastry cloth or board. Mix walnuts and jam in a small bowl; spread evenly over dough; roll up, jelly-roll fashion. (Be sure walnuts are chopped fine, or cookies will crack when rolled.) Wrap in wax paper or transparent wrap. Chill overnight, or until very firm.
5 When ready to bake, unwrap dough and slice into ¼-inch-thick rounds with a sharp knife; place, 1 inch apart, on greased cookie sheets.
6 Bake in moderate oven (375°) 10 minutes, or until firm. Remove from cookie sheets at once; cool completely on wire racks.

Chocolate Crisps

Crunchy and not too sweet—and perfect with a glass of milk or cup of tea.

Bake at 350° for 10 minutes.
Makes about 5 dozen

1¾ cups sifted all-purpose flour
 ¼ teaspoon baking soda
 ½ teaspoon salt
 ½ cup (1 stick) butter or margarine
 ¾ cup firmly packed brown sugar
  1 egg
  1 square unsweetened chocolate, melted
 ¾ teaspoon vanilla

1 Measure flour, soda, and salt into a sifter.
2 Cream butter or margarine with brown sugar until fluffy in a medium-size bowl; beat in egg, melted chocolate, and vanilla. Sift in flour mixture, blending well to make a soft dough.
3 Shape into 2 long rolls in wax paper; wrap tightly; chill overnight. When ready to bake, slice dough ⅛ inch thick; place on greased cookie sheets.
4 Bake in moderate oven (350°) 10 minutes, or until firm. Remove from cookie sheets; cool completely on wire racks.

How to be a clever cutup

Ball cookies will be even in size if you pat the dough into a long roll first, then divide it: First in half, then quarters, then eighths, and six-teenths, depending on what size cookie you want.

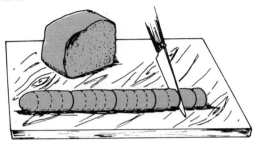

Shape double-good treats this easy way: Make up batches of vanilla and chocolate refrigerator cookie doughs, pat each into a rectangle, stack, chill well, and slice. What could be easier?

Juice cans make handy molds for refrigerator cookies. Pack dough in the can and chill, then, at baking time, remove the bottom of the can. (Use an opener that cuts a smooth edge.) Press against bottom to push out dough—just enough for one cookie at a time. Cutting against the can helps cookies keep their round shape.

Decorating, assembly-line style

With only one batch of dough, you can make a whole plateful of different-looking, different-tasting treats. Here's how: After shaping the dough, leave some plain, press others, criss-cross fashion, with a fork. Make a hollow in some with your thumb or the handle of a wooden spoon to fill with jam or jelly after baking, or top with a big walnut half.

Lemon Rounds

Dough keeps perfectly, so you can bake it in small batches, if you wish

Bake at 375° for 8 minutes.
Makes 4 dozen

1½ cups sifted all-purpose flour
½ teaspoon baking soda
½ teaspoon salt
½ cup vegetable shortening
1 cup sugar
1 egg
1 tablespoon lemon juice
2 teaspoons grated lemon rind
½ cup finely chopped pecans

1 Measure flour, soda, and salt into a sifter.
2 Cream shortening with sugar until fluffy in a medium-size bowl; beat in egg, lemon juice and rind, and pecans. Sift in flour mixture, blending well to make a soft dough.
3 Shape into 2 long rolls; wrap in wax paper; chill overnight. When ready to bake, slice dough ¼ inch thick; place on cookie sheets.
4 Bake in moderate oven (375°) 8 minutes, or until golden around edges. Remove from cookie sheets; cool completely on wire racks.

Pistachio Buttons

The tykes in the family will gobble these sweets up

Bake at 350° for 8 minutes.
Makes 16 dozen 1-inch cookies

2 cups sifted all-purpose flour
1 teaspoon baking powder
½ teaspoon salt
½ cup (1 stick) butter or margarine
¾ cup sugar
1 egg
1 teaspoon almond extract
¼ teaspoon vanilla
1 envelope (1 ounce) liquid unsweetened chocolate
⅓ cup finely chopped pistachio nuts
10 drops green food coloring

1 Sift flour, baking powder, and salt onto wax paper.
2 Cream butter or margarine with sugar until fluffy-light in a large bowl; beat in egg, almond extract, and vanilla. Stir in flour mixture, a third at a time, blending well to make a stiff dough.

Divide dough in half. Blend chocolate into one half; blend pistachio nuts and green food coloring into remaining half. Chill dough several hours, or overnight, until firm enough to handle. Divide each color into 4 even parts.
3 Roll green dough, one part at a time, into a log 8 inches long on a lightly floured pastry cloth or board; chill. Pat chocolate dough, one part at a time, into a rectangle 3 inches wide and 8 inches long. Roll around a green log; pinch edges to seal, then smooth out. Repeat with remaining doughs to make 4 rolls in all. Chill the rolls for at least an hour.
4 When ready to bake, slice each roll about ⅛ inch thick; place, ½ inch apart, on greased cookie sheets.
5 Bake in moderate oven (350°) 8 minutes, or until firm but not brown. Remove from cookie sheets; cool.

EVERYBODY'S FAVORITE BAR COOKIE

Best-Ever Brownies

"Irresistible" best describes these rich dark sweets with moist fudgy centers

Bake at 350° for 30 minutes.
Makes 16 squares

2 squares unsweetened chocolate
½ cup (1 stick) butter or margarine
2 eggs
1 cup sugar
½ teaspoon vanilla
½ cup sifted all-purpose flour
⅛ teaspoon salt
1 cup chopped walnuts

1 Melt chocolate with butter or margarine in a small saucepan.
2 Beat eggs until foamy in a large bowl; beat in sugar gradually until fluffy-thick. (This will take about 10 minutes.) Stir in vanilla and chocolate mixture, then fold in flour, salt, and walnuts. Spread in a greased baking pan, 8x8x2.
3 Bake in moderate oven (350°) 30 minutes, or until shiny and firm on top. Cool completely in pan on a wire rack; cut into 2-inch squares.

Choco-Butterscotch Squares

They're a triple treat with chocolate and walnuts between two chewy butterscotch layers

Bake at 375° for 40 minutes.
Makes 3 dozen

¾ cup sifted all-purpose flour
1 teaspoon salt
½ teaspoon baking soda
½ cup vegetable shortening (for butterscotch layers)
¾ cup firmly packed brown sugar
1 egg
1 teaspoon vanilla
1 cup corn flakes, crushed
1 cup quick-cooking rolled oats
1 package (6 ounces) butterscotch-flavor pieces
1 package (6 ounces) semisweet-chocolate pieces
1 tablespoon vegetable shortening (for chocolate layer)
1 can (4 ounces) walnuts, chopped (1 cup)
⅓ cup sweetened condensed milk (from a 14-ounce can)

1 Measure flour, salt, and soda into a sifter.
2 Cream the ½ cup shortening with brown sugar until fluffy in a large bowl; beat in egg and vanilla. Sift in flour mixture, blending well to make a soft dough.
3 Stir in crushed corn flakes, rolled oats, and butterscotch-flavor pieces. Spread half of the mixture evenly over bottom of a greased baking pan, 9x9x2; set remaining aside for Step 5.
4 Melt semisweet-chocolate pieces with the 1 tablespoon shortening in top of a double boiler over simmering water; remove from water. Stir in walnuts and sweetened condensed milk.
5 Spread over layer in pan, then spread with remaining butterscotch mixture.
6 Bake in moderate oven (375°) 40 minutes, or until firm and golden. Cool completely in pan on a wire rack. Cut into 36 squares.

Chocolate Trinkets

Part candy and part cookie, they go together and bake fast. Recipe makes lots, too

Bake at 350° for 15 minutes.
Makes about 5 dozen

2 packages (4 ounces each) sweet cooking chocolate

1 cup chopped walnuts
1 egg
½ cup sugar
1 can (3½ ounces) flaked coconut
8 candied red cherries

1 Heat chocolate in a baking pan, 9x9x2, while oven heats, 5 minutes, or just until soft. Spread in an even layer; sprinkle walnuts on top, pressing in lightly.
2 Beat egg until foamy in a small bowl; beat in sugar until well-blended; mix in coconut. Spread evenly on top of chocolate-walnut layer.
3 Cut candied cherries into eighths; place in even rows on top.
4 Bake in moderate oven (350°) 15 minutes, or just until coconut topping is set.
5 Cool in pan on a wire rack; cut into about-1-inch squares, but leave in pan. Chill until ready to serve, then cut again and remove.

Royal Scotch Shortbread

A tradition in many homes at Christmas time. Make ahead, for it tastes even richer if mellowed a few weeks

Bake at 300° for 45 minutes.
Makes about 4 dozen

1½ cups sifted all-purpose flour
1½ cups sifted 10X (confectioners' powdered) sugar
1 cup (2 sticks) butter or margarine

1 Sift flour and 10X sugar into medium-size bowl; cut in butter or margarine with pastry blender until mixture is crumbly. Work dough into a ball with hands and knead about 10 minutes.
2 Pat dough into a ¼-inch-thick rectangle, 14x12, on large ungreased cookie sheet; cut into 2-inch diamonds or squares with sharp knife but do not separate cookies.
3 Bake in slow oven (300°) 45 minutes, or until firm and delicately golden.
4 Recut cookies at marks and separate very carefully; remove from cookie sheets. Cool on wire racks. These cookies are very delicate, so handle carefully. Store with wax paper or transparent wrap between layers in container with tight-fitting cover.

Chocolate Shortbread

You don't have to hand these out twice—they'll be gone in a jiffy

Bake at 300° for 40 minutes.
Makes 8 dozen

1 cup (2 sticks) butter or margarine
½ cup very fine granulated sugar
2 squares semisweet chocolate, melted
2 cups sifted all-purpose flour
  Green decorating frosting from a pressurized can or a tube
  Candied red cherries, slivered

1 Cream butter or margarine with sugar until fluffy-light in a medium-size bowl. Beat in melted chocolate; stir in flour until well-blended.
2 Spread dough evenly in an ungreased baking pan, 13x9x2.
3 Bake in slow oven (300°) 40 minutes, or until firm. Cool slightly in pan on a wire rack, then cut lengthwise into 8 strips and crosswise into 12 to make about-1-inch squares. Cool completely. Decorate each with green frosting and a sliver of candied cherry.

Coffee-Date Bars

They're chewy with dates and nuts and have a pleasingly strong coffee flavor

Bake at 350° for 35 minutes.
Makes 3 dozen bars

1¼ cups sifted all-purpose flour
2 tablespoons instant coffee powder
1 teaspoon baking powder
¼ teaspoon salt
3 eggs
1 cup sugar
½ cup finely chopped pitted dates
½ cup coarsely chopped walnuts

1 Measure flour, instant coffee, baking powder, and salt into a sifter.
2 Beat eggs until light in a medium-size bowl; beat in sugar slowly; continue beating until thick, then beat in dates and walnuts. Sift flour mixture over and fold in. Spread in a greased baking pan, 13x9x2.
3 Bake in moderate oven (350°) 35 minutes, or until a wooden pick inserted in center comes out clean. Cool completely in pan on a wire rack; cut into bars.

Toffee-Raisin Bars

Lots of sugar, spice, and fruit go into these chewy cookies. They save time on busy days, for they take no fancy shaping

Bake at 375° for 20 minutes.
Makes 30 bars

2 cups sifted all-purpose flour
½ teaspoon baking soda
½ teaspoon ground nutmeg
½ teaspoon ground cinnamon
¼ teaspoon ground cloves
1 cup (2 sticks) butter or margarine
1¼ cups firmly packed brown sugar
2 eggs
2 tablespoons milk
1½ cups raisins

1 Measure flour, soda, nutmeg, cinnamon, and cloves into sifter.
2 Cream butter or margarine with brown sugar until fluffy in large bowl; beat in eggs and milk until well-blended.
3 Sift in dry ingredients, a third at a time, blending well to make a thick batter; stir in raisins. Spread evenly in lightly greased baking pan, 15x10x1.
4 Bake in moderate oven (375°) 20 minutes, or until browned around edges and top springs back when lightly pressed with fingertip. Cool in pan on wire rack; cut into bars or squares. (They're perfect, too, as a dinner dessert topped with sweetened whipped cream or ice cream.)

Date-Nut Chews

Bake 'em, then shape 'em. A little makes a lot.

Bake at 350° for 20 minutes.
Makes 12½ dozen

¾ cup sifted all-purpose flour
1 cup sugar
½ teaspoon baking powder
¼ teaspoon salt
1 cup chopped pitted dates
1 cup chopped walnuts
2 eggs
  10X (confectioners' powdered) sugar

1 Measure flour, sugar, baking powder, and salt into sifter.
2 Combine dates and walnuts in medium-size bowl; sift dry ingredients over; mix well.

3 Beat eggs until light in small bowl; stir into date-nut mixture; spread thinly in well-buttered baking pan, 15x10x1.
4 Bake in moderate oven (350°) 20 minutes, or until golden-brown.
5 Cool in pan 5 minutes; cut into strips, 1x2 inches; remove, one at a time, and roll into a log shape; slice crosswise into 1-inch-thick pieces; sprinkle with confectioners' (powdered) sugar.

Raspberry Chews

Little hints of walnut, raspberry, and coconut make these cookies delightful

Bake at 350° for 40 minutes.
Makes about 8 dozen

¾ cup (1½ sticks) butter or margarine
¾ cup sugar
2 eggs, separated
1½ cups sifted all-purpose flour
1 cup chopped walnuts
1 cup raspberry preserves
½ cup flaked coconut

1 Cream butter or margarine with ¼ cup of the sugar until fluffy-light in a medium-size bowl; beat in egg yolks.
2 Stir in flour until blended. Spread evenly in an ungreased baking pan, 13x9x2.
3 Bake in moderate oven (350°) 15 minutes, or until golden; remove from oven.
4 While layer bakes, beat egg whites until foamy-white and double in volume in a small bowl; beat in remaining ½ cup sugar until meringue stands in firm peaks; fold in walnuts.
5 Spread raspberry preserves over layer in pan; sprinkle with coconut. Spread meringue over raspberry-coconut layer.
6 Bake in moderate oven (350°) 25 minutes, or until lightly golden. Cool completely in pan on a wire rack. Cut into about-1-inch squares.

Date Accordions

So tasty, it's hard not to take another and another

Bake at 350° for 25 minutes.
Makes about 6 dozen

¾ cup sifted all-purpose flour
½ teaspoon baking powder

¼ teaspoon salt
3 eggs
1 cup sugar (for dough)
2 tablespoons orange juice
1 package (8 ounces) pitted dates, chopped
1 cup chopped pecans
¼ cup chopped candied orange peel
Sugar (for coating)
Canned or refrigerated ready-to-spread vanilla frosting
Green decorating gel in plastic tube

1 Sift flour, baking powder, and salt onto wax paper.
2 Beat eggs until foamy-light in a large bowl; slowly beat in the 1 cup sugar; continue beating until mixture is fluffy-thick. Stir in orange juice.
3 Fold in flour mixture, dates, pecans, and orange peel. Spread evenly in a greased baking pan, 13x9x2.
4 Bake in moderate oven (350°) 25 minutes, or until golden and top springs back when lightly pressed with fingertip. Cool in pan on a wire rack 15 minutes.
5 Cut lengthwise into 9 strips and crosswise into 8 to make 72 pieces, about 1x1½. Roll each in sugar in a pie plate to coat generously. (Cookies are soft and will roll into a log.)
6 Top each with an accordion-shape ribbon of vanilla frosting pressed through a pastry tube, then cover frosting with green decorating gel. Let stand on wire racks until frosting is firm.

Coconut Chews

One bite and you'll taste the delicious fruits and walnut

Bake at 300° for 30 minutes.
Makes 4 dozen

1 egg
½ cup sugar
1 teaspoon vanilla
1 cup finely chopped pitted dates
1 package (7 ounces) cookie coconut
⅓ cup finely chopped candied red cherries
⅓ cup chopped walnuts
Red and green food colorings

1 Beat egg until foamy in a medium-size bowl; beat in sugar until fluffy-thick. Stir in vanilla, dates, ¾ cup of the coconut, cherries, and walnuts. Spoon into a greased baking pan, 9x9x2.
2 Bake in slow oven (300°) 30 minutes, or until
(continued)

golden and top springs back when lightly pressed with fingertip. Cool in pan on a wire rack 15 minutes, or just until warm.
3 While cookies cool, divide remaining coconut into two small jars with lids. Add a drop or two of red or green food colorings to each; shake until coconut is evenly tinted. Spread out on sheets of wax paper.
4 Cut cookies lengthwise into 8 strips and crosswise into 6 to make 48 pieces. Roll each into a ball between palms of hands, then roll in tinted coconut to coat generously. Cool completely on wire racks.

Cranberry Crunch Bars

Gift-giving is easy with the crunchables

Bake at 400° for 35 minutes.
Makes 8 dozen small bars

1¾ cups sifted all-purpose flour
¾ teaspoon salt
1½ teaspoons ground cinnamon
1¼ cups firmly packed light brown sugar
2 cups quick-cooking rolled oats
1 cup (2 sticks) butter or margarine
1 cup finely chopped walnuts
½ cup granulated sugar
2 tablespoons cornstarch
2 jars (14 ounces each) cranberry-orange relish
1 egg
1 tablespoon water
10X (confectioners' powdered) sugar

1 Sift flour, salt, and cinnamon into a large bowl; stir in brown sugar and rolled oats. Cut in butter or margarine with a pastry blender until mixture is crumbly; stir in walnuts. Press half of mixture evenly over bottom of a lightly greased baking pan, 13x9x2.
2 Bake in hot oven (400°) 5 minutes; cool slightly on a wire rack.
3 While layer bakes, mix granulated sugar and cornstarch in a medium-size saucepan; stir in cranberry relish. Cook slowly, stirring constantly, until mixture thickens and boils 3 minutes. Spread evenly over partly baked layer in pan. Sprinkle remaining rolled-oats mixture over top; press down firmly with hand.
4 Beat egg well in a cup; stir in water. Brush lightly over crumb mixture.
5 Bake in hot oven (400°) 30 minutes, or until firm and golden. Cool completely in pan on a wire rack.

6 Cut in quarters lengthwise, then crosswise; lift each piece from pan with a pancake turner. Cut each of these pieces in half crosswise, then in thirds lengthwise to make 6 small bars. Dust lightly with 10X sugar.

Frosted Jewel Sticks

Make 'em and bake 'em—if you've done it once, you'll have to do it again

Bake at 300° for 2½ hours.
Makes about 4 dozen

4 cups mixed candied fruits
2 cans (3 ounces each) pecans, chopped
4 cups sifted all-purpose flour
2 teaspoons baking powder
1½ teaspoons salt
1 cup (2 sticks) butter or margarine
1½ cups sugar
4 eggs
½ cup milk
½ teaspoon almond extract
BASIC BUTTER CREAM (recipe follows)

1 Line a baking pan, 15x10x1, with a double thickness of brown paper; grease paper.
2 Combine candied fruits and pecans in a large bowl.
3 Sift flour, baking powder, and salt onto wax paper; sprinkle 1 cup over fruit mixture; toss lightly.
4 Cream butter or margarine with sugar until fluffy in a large bowl; beat in eggs, 1 at a time. Blend in remaining flour mixture, adding alternately with milk; stir in almond extract, then fold in fruit mixture. Spoon into prepared pan, spreading evenly.
5 Bake in slow oven (300°) 2½ hours, or until a wooden pick inserted in center comes out clean.
6 Let cool completely in pan on a wire rack. Loosen around edge with knife; turn out onto rack; peel off paper. Frost with BASIC BUTTER CREAM and sprinkle with grated semisweet chocolate, if you wish. Cut into sticks, each about 3x1.

BASIC BUTTER CREAM
Cream ½ cup (1 stick) butter or margarine until soft in a medium-size bowl; beat in 1 package (1 pound) 10X (confectioners' powdered) sugar, alternately with mixture of 3 tablespoons milk and 1 teaspoon vanilla until smooth. Makes 2 cups.

Good things do come in small packages. And **Peanut Butter Bars** are among the best.

Peanut Butter Bars

These moist chewy bar cookies, drizzled with glaze then with chocolate, will be a favorite with the kids

Bake at 350° for 35 minutes.
Makes three dozen

1 cup crunchy peanut butter
⅔ cup butter or margarine, softened
1 teaspoon vanilla
2 cups firmly packed light brown sugar
3 eggs
1 cup sifted all-purpose flour
½ teaspoon salt
¾ cup sifted 10X (confectioners' powdered) sugar
2 teaspoons water
¼ cup semisweet chocolate pieces (from a 6-ounce package)
1 teaspoon vegetable shortening

1 Combine peanut butter, butter or margarine and vanilla in a large bowl; beat with electric beater until well-blended; beat in sugar until light and fluffy; beat in eggs, one at a time.
2 Stir in flour and salt just until well-blended; spread batter in a greased 13x9x2-inch baking pan.
3 Bake in moderate oven (350°) 35 minutes, or until center springs back when lightly touched with fingertip. Remove pan from oven to wire rack; cool slightly.
4 Combine 10X sugar with water in a small bowl; stir until smooth; drizzle from a spoon over still-warm cookies in pan; swirl with bowl of spoon to make a random pattern.
5 Melt chocolate with shortening over simmering water in top of double boiler. Drizzle over the white glaze for a black-and-white pattern. When cool, using a sharp knife, cut into 36 rectangles. Carefully lift out of pan with spatula.

Lebkuchen Squares

Each sweet and chewy cherry-topped cookie is rich with spice, almonds, and raisins

Bake at 350° for 30 minutes.
Makes 6 dozen

1 cup honey
¾ cup firmly packed brown sugar
1 egg
1 teaspoon grated lemon rind
3 tablespoons lemon juice
2 cups sifted all-purpose flour
1 tablespoon pumpkin-pie spice
½ teaspoon baking soda
¼ teaspoon salt
½ cup golden raisins
½ cup chopped blanched almonds
1 cup sifted 10X (confectioners' powdered) sugar
18 candied green cherries, halved
18 candied red cherries, halved

1 Heat honey to boiling in small saucepan; pour into large bowl; cool completely. Stir in brown sugar, egg, lemon rind, and 1 tablespoon lemon juice. (Save remaining 2 tablespoons for Step 5.)
2 Sift dry ingredients into medium-size bowl; stir in raisins and almonds. Gradually stir into honey mixture, blending well. Chill overnight to blend flavors.
3 Divide dough and spread evenly into 2 greased baking pans, each 9x9x2.
4 Bake in moderate oven (350°) 30 minutes, or until firm.
5 While cookies bake, stir saved 2 tablespoons lemon juice into 10X sugar until smooth in small bowl.
6 Set pans of hot cookies on wire racks; press 36 cherry halves, cut side down, in 6 even rows on top in each pan; drizzle frosting over. Cool cookies completely in pans, then cut each panful into 36 squares.

Walnut Frosties

Cut this triple-layer confection into bitsy squares, for it's rich and sweet

Bake at 350° for 35 minutes.
Makes 3 dozen

1 cup sifted all-purpose flour (for crust)
2 tablespoons 10X (confectioners' powdered) sugar
½ cup (1 stick) butter or margarine
2 eggs

1 cup firmly packed brown sugar
2 tablespoons all-purpose flour (for topping)
½ teaspoon baking powder
⅛ teaspoon salt
1 cup coarsely chopped walnuts
½ cup flaked coconut
ORANGE BUTTER CREAM (recipe follows)

1 Combine 1 cup flour and 10X sugar in medium-size bowl; cream in butter or margarine until well-blended. Pat firmly and evenly into bottom of an ungreased baking pan, 9x9x2.
2 Bake in moderate oven (350°) 10 minutes; remove and let cool on wire rack 5 minutes. (Leave oven heat on.)
3 Beat eggs slightly in medium-size bowl; stir in brown sugar until well-blended, then 2 tablespoons flour, baking powder, and salt. Fold in walnuts and coconut; pour over crust.
4 Bake 25 minutes longer, or until top is firm; cool completely in pan. Frost with ORANGE BUTTER CREAM; cut into 36 tiny squares. Top each with a walnut half, if you wish.

ORANGE BUTTER CREAM

Beat 2 tablespoons melted butter or margarine and 1½ teaspoons orange juice into 1¼ cups sifted 10X (confectioners' powdered) sugar until smooth and creamy in small bowl; stir in 1½ teaspoons grated orange rind. Makes about ½ cup.

POPULAR SHAPED COOKIES

Lemon-Nutmeg Meltaway Cookies

Truly melt-in-the-mouth delicacies, with a fragile lemony aroma

Bake at 325° for 15 minutes.
Makes 64 single cookies or 32 double cookies.

1 cup sifted cake flour
½ cup cornstarch
¼ teaspoon salt
½ teaspoon ground nutmeg
10 tablespoons (1 stick plus 2 tablespoons) unsalted butter or margarine, softened
½ cup 10X (confectioners') sugar
2 teaspoons grated lemon rind

1 Sift flour, cornstarch, salt and nutmeg onto wax paper.

An ever popular cooky is one based on peanut butter. For a variation on **Peanut-Butter Crisscrosses,** after you flatten the cookies, press on peanut halves.

2 Beat butter (or margarine), sugar and lemon rind in a medium-size bowl with electric mixer until light and fluffy.

3 Add sifted dry ingredients to butter mixture. Beat on low speed, scraping bowl, until mixture is smooth. Roll dough by measuring teaspoonfuls into balls. Place on ungreased cookie sheet; flatten slightly to 1¼-inch circles with bottom of glass dipped in 10X sugar.

4 Bake in a slow oven (325°) for 15 minutes or until cookies have turned a very pale golden-brown around the edges.

5 Cool 2 minutes on the cookie sheet, then transfer to a wire rack and cool completely. Pack into airtight containers and store up to 1 week.

Note: Cookies can be put together in pairs as follows: Cook ½ cup apricot preserves with 1 tablespoon sugar in a small saucepan for 2 minutes, stirring constantly. Cool, then spread just enough of the mixture between pairs of cookies to hold firmly.

Peanut-Butter Crisscrosses

Orange juice adds a subtle new flavor to these melt-in-your-mouth favorites

Bake at 375° for 12 minutes.
Makes about 5 dozen

 2 *cups sifted all-purpose flour*
¾ *teaspoon baking soda*
½ *teaspoon baking powder*
¼ *teaspoon salt*
½ *cup vegetable shortening*
½ *cup peanut butter*
½ *cup firmly packed brown sugar*
½ *cup granulated sugar*
 1 *egg*
¼ *cup orange juice*

1 Measure flour, soda, baking powder, and salt into a sifter.

2 Cream shortening and peanut butter with brown and granulated sugars until fluffy in a large bowl; beat in egg. Sift in flour mixture,

(continued)

adding alternately with orange juice and blending well to make a stiff dough. Chill until firm enough to handle.

3 Roll dough, a teaspoonful at a time, into balls; place, 3 inches apart, on ungreased cookie sheets; flatten, crisscross fashion, with a fork.

4 Bake in moderate oven (375°) 12 minutes, or until golden. Remove from cookie sheets; cool completely on wire racks.

Coconut Gingeroons

The crunchy surface of these cookies is like that of gingersnaps, while the rather soft centers suggest coconut macaroons

Bake at 375° for 15 minutes.
Makes about 3½ dozen.

2 cups sifted *all-purpose flour*
½ teaspoon baking soda
1½ teaspoons ground ginger
½ teaspoon ground cinnamon
½ teaspoon ground coriander
⅛ teaspoon salt
½ cup (1 stick) unsalted butter or margarine softened
½ cup firmly packed light brown sugar
¼ cup molasses
1 egg
2 cans (4 ounces each) shredded coconut, chopped (2 cups)
½ cup granulated sugar

1 Sift flour, baking soda, ginger, cinnamon, coriander and salt onto wax paper.

2 Beat the butter (or margarine) in a medium-size bowl with electric mixer. While beating, sprinkle in the brown sugar with your fingers, removing lumps if any. Add molasses and egg and continue to beat until mixture is fluffy.

3 Stir in the flour mixture until smooth; stir in the coconut. Chill several hours.

4 Roll dough by level tablespoonfuls between your palms to form balls. Quickly dip one side into water, then into the granulated sugar. Place sugar side up on a large foil-covered cookie sheet. Flatten slightly.

5 Bake in a moderate oven (375°) for 15 minutes or until cookies are lightly browned. Transfer to wire racks; cool completely. Pack into airtight containers and store up to 2 weeks.

Snowballs

Buttery snow-white puffs that literally melt in your mouth—and one just teases you into having another

Bake at 325° for 20 minutes.
Makes 4 dozen

½ cup (1 stick) butter or margarine
3 tablespoons 10X (confectioners' powdered) sugar
1 cup sifted all-purpose flour
1 cup finely chopped pecans
10X (confectioners' powdered) sugar

1 Cream butter or margarine and 3 tablespoons 10X sugar until fluffy in medium-size bowl; stir in flour gradually, then pecans until well-blended. Chill several hours, or until firm enough to handle.

2 Roll dough, a teaspoonful at a time, into marble-size balls between palms of hands; place, 2 inches apart, on ungreased cookie sheets.

3 Bake in slow oven (325°) 20 minutes, or until lightly golden.

4 Cool on cookie sheets 5 minutes; remove carefully. Roll in 10X sugar in pie plate while still warm to make a generous white coating; cool completely on wire racks. Store with wax paper or transparent wrap between layers in container with tight-fitting cover.

Chocolate Snowballs

They're sugary-white outside, dark chocolate inside. Bake some to pack for gifts

Bake at 350° for 8 minutes.
Makes about 5 dozen

2 cups sifted all-purpose flour
1 teaspoon baking powder
½ teaspoon salt
¼ teaspoon baking soda
¾ cup (1½ sticks) butter or margarine
¾ cup firmly packed brown sugar
2 squares unsweetened chocolate, melted
1 egg
1 teaspoon vanilla
¼ cup milk
10X (confectioners' powdered) sugar

1 Measure dry ingredients into sifter.

2 Cream butter or margarine with brown sugar until light in medium-size bowl; beat in melted chocolate, egg, vanilla, and milk. Sift in dry ingredients, a little at a time, blending well to make a stiff dough. Chill overnight, or until firm enough to handle.

3 Roll dough, a teaspoonful at a time, into marble-size balls; place about 2 inches apart on ungreased cookie sheets.

4 Bake in moderate oven (350°) 8 minutes, or until tops are crackled. Remove carefully from cookie sheets; roll in 10X sugar while still hot. Cool on wire racks, then roll again in 10X sugar to make a generous white coating.

Butternut Crescents

A cookie lover's dream come true, for these are nut-packed, melt-away morsels

Bake at 300° for 20 minutes.
Makes about 6 dozen

1 cup (2 sticks) butter or margarine
¼ cup 10X (confectioners' powdered) sugar (for dough)
1 tablespoon water
2 teaspoons vanilla
2 cups sifted all-purpose flour
1 cup finely chopped pecans
   10X (confectioners' powdered) sugar (for coating)

1 Melt butter or margarine in small suacepan; remove from heat. Stir in ¼ cup 10X sugar, water, and vanilla; gradually blend in flour, then pecans, to make a pastrylike dough.

2 Pinch off dough, about a teaspoonful at a time, and roll lightly between palms of hands into fingerlike strips about 2 inches long. Place on ungreased cookie sheets; curve into crescents.

3 Bake in slow oven (300°) 20 minutes, or until delicately golden.

4 Remove carefully from cookie sheets; dust with 10X sugar while still hot. Cool on wire rack, then dust again with 10X sugar to make a generous white coating.

BUTTERNUT MOONS

Shape half of the dough for BUTTERNUT CRESCENTS into small balls, like fat full moons, then bake the same as CRESCENTS. Decorate cooled balls with a dollop of PECAN COCOA CREAM (recipe follows); press a pecan half into soft frosting.

PECAN-COCOA CREAM

Blend ¼ cup unsifted 10X (confectioners' powdered) sugar, 2 teaspoons dry cocoa, 2 teaspoons milk, and 1 teaspoon melted butter or margarine until creamy-smooth in 1-cup measure. Makes enough for 3 dozen.

Cookie-Jar Gingersnaps

A batch of these will rarely go far—small and large fingers will keep removing them

Bake at 350° for 12 to 15 minutes.
Makes about 4 dozen

2 cups sifted all-purpose flour
1 tablespoon ground ginger
2 teaspoons baking soda
1 teaspoon ground cinnamon
½ teaspoon salt
¾ cup vegetable shortening
1 cup sugar
1 egg, unbeaten
¼ cup molasses
   Granulated sugar

1 Measure flour, ginger, baking soda, cinnamon, and salt into sifter; sift 2 times onto wax paper; return to sifter.

2 Cream shortening until soft in medium-size bowl; add sugar gradually, creaming after each addition until mixture is well-blended.

3 Beat in egg and molasses.

4 Sift dry ingredients over creamed mixture; blend well.

5 Form teaspoonfuls of dough into small balls by rolling them lightly, one at a time, between palms of hands. Roll dough balls in granulated sugar to cover entire outside surface; place 2 inches apart on ungreased cookie sheets.

6 Bake in moderate oven (35u°) 12 to 15 minutes, or until tops are slightly rounded, crackly, and lightly browned.

7 Run spatula under cookies to loosen from sheets; cool on wire racks.

Shortbread Cookies

Use this basic recipe and any one of the shape-styles on these pages

Bake at 300° for 25 minutes.
Makes about 5 dozen

1 cup (2 sticks) butter or margarine
½ cup sugar
½ teaspoon lemon extract
2½ cups sifted all-purpose flour
   DECORATOR'S ICING (recipe follows)

1 Beat butter or margarine with sugar until fluffy-light in a large bowl. Beat in lemon extract. Stir in flour, a third at a time, blending well to make a stiff dough.

(continued)

2 Knead in bowl 10 to 15 minutes, or until smooth. Wrap in wax paper or transparent wrap; chill several hours, or until firm. (Overnight is even better.)

3 Roll dough, a rounded teaspoonful at a time, between palms of hands, into 1-inch balls. Place, 2 inches apart, on ungreased large cookie sheets. Flatten with a floured cookie mold or a small glass to a ¼-inch thickness.

4 Bake in slow oven (300°) 25 minutes, or until firm and lightly golden. Remove from cookie sheets to wire racks; cool completely. Attach a small round tip to a cake-decorating set. Fill with DECORATOR'S ICING. Pipe design on cookies, following patterned tops; or glaze entire top with icing. Let stand until design is firm. Store in a tightly covered container.

DECORATOR'S ICING

Combine 1 cup 10X (confectioners' powdered) sugar, 2½ teaspoons water, and 10 drops yellow food coloring in a small bowl, mixing until smooth. Makes about ⅓ cup icing, or enough for 6 dozen 1½-inch cookies.

Chocolate Crinkle Puffs

A shower of sugar makes these fudgy charmers crackle prettily on top as they bake. Tuck a few into lunch boxes for a surprise

Bake at 350° for 8 minutes.
Makes about 5 dozen

2 cups sifted all-purpose flour
1 teaspoon baking powder
½ teaspoon salt
¼ teaspoon baking soda
¾ cup (1½ sticks) butter or margarine
¾ cup firmly packed brown sugar
2 squares unsweetened chocolate, melted
1 egg
1 teaspoon vanilla
¼ cup milk
Granulated sugar

1 Measure flour, baking powder, salt, and soda into sifter.

2 Cream butter or margarine with brown sugar until fluffy in medium-size bowl; beat in melted chocolate, egg, vanilla, and milk.

3 Sift in dry ingredients, a third at a time, blending well to make a stiff dough.

4 Roll dough, a teaspoonful at a time, into marble-size balls; roll in granulated sugar; place about 2 inches apart on ungreased cookie sheets.

5 Bake in moderate oven (350°) 8 minutes, or until tops are crackled. Remove carefully from cookie sheets; cool on wire racks.

Chocolate Walnut Wafers

These fudgy rounds sparkle prettily with a sugary coating—and shaping's so easy

Bake at 350° for 12 minutes.
Makes 4 dozen

2 cups sifted all-purpose flour
1 teaspoon baking powder
½ teaspoon salt
¼ teaspoon baking soda
¾ cup (1½ sticks) butter or margarine
¾ cup firmly packed brown sugar
2 squares unsweetened chocolate, melted
1 egg
1 teaspoon vanilla
¼ cup milk
Granulated sugar
Walnut halves

1 Measure flour, baking powder, salt, and baking soda into sifter.

2 Cream butter or margarine and brown sugar until fluffy in medium-size bowl; beat in melted chocolate, egg, vanilla, and milk. Sift in dry ingredients, a third at a time, blending well to make a soft dough. Chill several hours, or until firm enough to handle.

3 Roll dough, a heaping teaspoonful at a time, into marble-size balls between palms of hands; roll in granulated sugar in pie plate. Place, 3 inches apart, on ungreased cookie sheets; flatten to ¼-inch thickness with bottom of glass. Top each with a walnut half.

4 Bake in moderate oven (350°) 12 minutes, or until firm. Remove carefully from cookie sheets; cool on wire racks. Store in container with tight-fitting cover.

Gift-giving needn't be expensive, if you know how to cook and mail. **Chocolate Walnut Wafers** are perfect for sitting on the sideboard or for mailing to a friend.

Store your cookies—right!

Place soft cookies in a canister or box with a tight cover to keep moisture in. Short on containers? Seal cookies in a transparent bag and tuck away in the cupboard. To keep crisp cookies crisp, or fancy cut-outs from breaking, layer with transparent wrap, foil, or wax paper between in a large shallow pan or roaster or on a tray. Bar cookies can stay right in their baking pan tightly covered with foil.

Four basic types of cookies: a frosted cut-out, a refrigerator pinwheel, a drop cookie crowned with a cherry and a nut-filled spritz wreath.

How To Pack Cookies for Mailing

Containers—For sending cookies overseas, use empty metal coffee or shortening cans that come with plastic lids, or metal boxes that are available in variety or housewares stores. Sturdy plastic containers are a satisfactory choice if the cookies are being sent only a short distance. For a bright holiday look, it's fun to cover the container with gaily colored wallpaper or self-adhesive plastic.

Packing—Wrap cookies in pairs, flat sides together, in pieces of foil long enough to allow a generous overlap; seal each with cellophane tape. Cushion the bottom of the container with a layer of crumpled foil and arrange the cookies on top, packing them in as tightly as possible. Stuff any holes between with more foil to keep the cookies from bouncing about. Affix the lid and seal with tape.

Wrapping—Cover the container with a layer of corrugated cardboard, then wrap in a double layer of brown paper. Tie securely with twine or heavy string and affix an address label (typed or printed) on one side only.

Butternuts

The more you make, the more your children will want you to make more

Bake at 325° for 15 minutes.
Makes about 8 dozen

¾ cup (1½ sticks) butter or margarine
½ cup sifted 10X (confectioners' powdered) sugar
¼ teaspoon salt
1¾ cups sifted all-purpose flour
 1 package (6 ounces) butterscotch-flavor pieces (1 cup)
 1 cup finely chopped pecans
   RUM GLAZE (recipe follows)
   Pecan halves
   Candied red cherries, halved

1 Cream butter or margarine with 10X sugar and salt in a medium-size bowl; blend in flour until smooth. Stir in butterscotch pieces and pecans.
2 Shape dough, a scant teaspoonful at a time, into balls between palms of hands; place, 1 inch apart, on large ungreased cookie sheets.
3 Bake in slow oven (325°) 15 minutes, or until firm but not brown. Remove from cookie sheets to wire racks; let cool completely.
4 Make RUM GLAZE. Place cookies in a single layer on wire racks set over wax paper; spoon glaze over each to cover completely. (Scrape glaze that drips onto paper back into bowl and beat until smooth before using again.) Decorate each with a pecan or candied-cherry half. Let cookies stand until glaze is firm.

RUM GLAZE
Combine 2 cups sifted 10X (confectioners' powdered) sugar and ¼ cup light rum in a medium-size bowl; beat until smooth. Makes ¾ cup.

Almond Wreaths

Decorate the wreath with red and green cherries

Bake at 300° for 20 minutes.
Makes about 5 dozen

2 cans (5 ounces each) whole blanched almonds
2 cups sifted all-purpose flour
1 cup (2 sticks) butter or margarine
1 cup 10X (confectioners' powdered) sugar
2 tablespoons lemon juice
  Red and green candied cherries

1 Chop or grind almonds very fine; mix with flour in a medium-size bowl.
2 Cream butter or margarine with 10X sugar until fluffy-light in a large bowl; beat in lemon juice.
3 Stir in flour mixture, a third at a time, blending well to make a soft dough. Chill several hours, or overnight, until firm enough to handle.
4 Roll dough, a heaping teaspoonful at a time, into balls between palms of hands. Place, 2 inches apart, on large ungreased cookie sheets.
5 Flatten each ball to a 2-inch round with palm of hand; press a hole in center with tip of wooden-spoon handle. Decorate each with half a red cherry and slivers of green cherry.
6 Bake in slow oven (300°) 20 minutes, or until firm but not brown. Remove carefully from cookie sheets to wire racks; cool completely.

Sugar-Crusted Chocolate Pretzels

Cookies with a deep chocolate flavor and crunchy sugary surface—which gets crunchier with storage

Bake at 350° for 12 minutes.
Makes about 6 dozen.

1¾ cups sifted all-purpose flour
½ cup unsweetened cocoa powder
 1 teaspoon baking powder
⅛ teaspoon salt
½ cup (1 stick) unsalted butter or margarine, softened
¾ cup sugar
 2 eggs
 1 tablespoon dark rum
 1 teaspoon water
¼ cup large-crystal decorating sugar
   OR: 12 sugar cubes crushed with a rolling pin

1 Sift flour, cocoa, baking powder and salt onto wax paper.
2 Beat butter (or margarine), sugar, 1 egg and rum in a medium-size bowl with electric mixer at high speed until very light and fluffy. Stir in the dry ingredients, mixing well until soft dough forms. Wrap dough in foil or plastic and chill for at least 1 hour.
3 Divide dough in thirds. Work with 1 part; keep others refrigerated. Using 1 level tablespoonful of dough, roll to a 15-inch rope with palms of hands. Cut into three 5-inch pieces. Roll each piece to 7 inches, tapering ends. Twist into pretzel shape. Repeat with remaining dough.

(continued)

4 Beat remaining egg with the water in a small bowl. Brush over the pretzels, then sprinkle on the decorating sugar.
5 Bake in a moderate oven (350°) for 12 minutes or until firm. Cool on wire racks. Pack in airtight containers with foil or plastic between layers. Store up to 1½ weeks.

No-Bake Chocolate Truffles

So easy to make, they are perfect for the young cook

Makes 6 dozen

1 package (6 ounces) semisweet-chocolate pieces
½ cup orange juice
3 tablespoons light rum
1 package (8½ ounces) chocolate wafer cookies, crushed
3 cups sifted 10X (confectioners' powdered) sugar
1 cup very finely chopped walnuts
1 container (4 ounces) chocolate decorating sprinkles
Red candied cherries

1 Melt chocolate pieces in top of a double boiler over simmering water; remove from heat. Blend in orange juice and rum; stir in chocolate cooky crumbs, 2 cups of the 10X sugar, and nuts until well-mixed. Cover; chill about 2 hours, or until stiff enough to handle.
2 Roll dough, a rounded teaspoonful at a time, into balls between palms of hands. Roll balls in chocolate sprinkles to coat generously, pressing firmly as you roll. Place on a tray; cover; chill several hours or overnight.
3 Blend remaining 1 cup 10X sugar with enough water in a small bowl to make a smooth thick glaze. Dip chocolate balls halfway into glaze to coat tops. Decorate with candied cherry pieces; place on wire racks until glaze is set.

Ginger Wafers

A couple of bites, and the wafer disappears

Bake at 350° for 13 minutes.
Makes about 4 dozen

2 cups sifted all-purpose flour
3 teaspoons ground ginger
2 teaspoons baking soda
1 teaspoon ground cinnamon
½ teaspoon salt
¾ cup (1½ sticks) butter or margarine
1 cup sugar (for dough)
1 egg
¼ cup molasses
Sugar (for coating)

1 Sift flour, ginger, soda, cinnamon, and salt onto wax paper.
2 Cream butter or margarine with the 1 cup sugar until fluffy in a medium-size bowl; beat in egg and molasses.
3 Stir in flour mixture, a third at a time, until well-blended.
4 Roll dough, a teaspoonful at a time, into small balls between palms of hands; roll each in sugar in a pie plate to coat generously. Place, 2 inches apart, on ungreased cookie sheets.
5 Bake in moderate oven (350°) 13 minutes, or until tops are crackled. Remove from cookie sheets to wire racks. Cool completely.

Meltaways

They look substantial enough, yet they melt in your mouth

Bake at 350° for 15 minutes.
Makes about 3 dozen double cookies

1 cup (2 sticks) butter or margarine
1½ cups sifted 10X (confectioners' powdered) sugar
1½ cups sifted all-purpose flour
1 teaspoon vanilla
¾ cup finely chopped walnuts
1 can vanilla creamy-type frosting
Red, yellow, or green food coloring

1 Beat butter or margarine with ½ cup of the 10X sugar until fluffy-light in a large bowl. Stir in flour, vanilla, and nuts, blending well to make a stiff dough.
2 Roll dough, a level teaspoonful at a time, into balls between palms of hands. Place, one inch apart, on lightly greased cookie sheets.
3 Bake in moderate oven (350°) 15 minutes, or until firm. Remove carefully from cookie sheets; while still hot, roll in 10X sugar. Cool on wire racks; roll again in 10X sugar to make a generous white coating.
4 Spoon frosting into a small bowl. Tint pink, green, or yellow with food coloring. Attach a small round tip to a cake-decorating set; fill tube with tinted frosting. Pipe frosting onto flat sides of half the cookies (or spread frosting with a small spatula). Press flat sides of remaining

cookies to frosted cookies. Stand cookies on edge on wire racks until frosting is firm. Or divide frosting evenly into 3 small bowls; tint pink, yellow, and green. Fill cake-decorating set with one color at a time, washing set as you change colors.

Swedish Candy Nuggets

Chocolate-candy pieces or bright gumdrops go into the center of each of these crunchy almond cookies

Bake at 375° for 15 minutes.
Makes 3 dozen

½ cup (1 stick) butter or margarine
¼ cup firmly packed brown sugar
 1 egg, separated
½ teaspoon vanilla
 1 cup sifted all-purpose flour
¼ teaspoon salt
½ cup coarsely chopped almonds
¼ cup semisweet-chocolate pieces
18 small red gumdrops

1 Cream butter or margarine and brown sugar until fluffy in medium-size bowl; beat in egg yolk and vanilla. (Save egg white for next step.) Sift in flour and salt gradually, stirring until well-blended. Chill several hours, or until firm enough to handle.
2 Beat saved egg white with a fork until foamy in pie plate; place almonds in second pie plate.
3 Roll dough, a heaping teaspoonful at a time, into marble-size balls between palms of hands. Roll each in egg white, then in almonds. Place, 3 inches apart, on greased cookie sheets.
4 Make a hollow in center of each ball with tip of finger or handle of wooden spoon. Fill hollows of half with 3 each semisweet-chocolate pieces, pointed ends up; fill each of remaining with a single gumdrop.
5 Bake in moderate oven (375°) 15 minutes, or until firm and lightly golden. Remove carefully from cookie sheets; cool on wire racks. Store in container with tight-fitting cover.

Robin's Nests

A small nest for a fondant egg

Bake at 350° for 12 minutes.
Makes 3 dozen

2¼ cups sifted all-purpose flour
 1 cup (2 sticks) butter or margarine

½ cup firmly packed brown sugar
 2 eggs, separated
1½ teaspoons vanilla
1½ cups finely chopped walnuts
 FONDANT EGGS (recipe follows)

1 Sift flour onto wax paper.
2 Cream butter or margarine with brown sugar until fluffy-light in a medium-size bowl; beat in egg yolks and vanilla. Stir in flour, half at a time, blending well to make a stiff dough.
3 Beat egg whites until foamy in a pie plate; sprinkle walnuts on wax paper.
4 Roll dough, 1 teaspoonful at a time, into balls between palms of hands; roll each in egg white, then into walnuts to coat all over. Place, 2 inches apart, on ungreased large cookie sheets. Press a hollow in center of each with fingertip.
5 Bake in moderate oven (350°) 12 minutes, or until firm and lightly golden. Remove from cookie sheets to wire racks; cool completely. Place a FONDANT EGG in each "nest."

FONDANT EGGS
Cream 2 tablespoons butter or margarine until soft in a small bowl; stir in 3 tablespoons light corn syrup, ½ teaspoon almond extract, and 2 cups sifted 10X (confectioners' powdered) sugar until smooth. Knead in 2 drops blue food coloring and 1 drop green food coloring to tint robin's-egg blue. Pinch off fondant, ½ teaspoonful at a time, and roll into egg shapes between palms of hands. Makes 3 dozen tiny candy eggs.

Peppermint Bonbons

After dinner delicacies that will be enjoyed by everyone

Bake at 350° for 12 minutes.
Makes about 4 dozen

 2 cups sifted all-purpose flour
½ teaspoon baking powder
½ teaspoon salt
½ cup (1 stick) butter or margarine
½ cup sugar
 1 egg
 1 square unsweetened chocolate, melted
 1 teaspoon vanilla
 PEPPERMINT GLAZE (recipe follows)

1 Sift flour, baking powder, and salt onto wax paper.
2 Cream butter or margarine with sugar until fluffy-light in a large bowl; beat in egg, choco-
(continued)

late, and vanilla. Stir in flour mixture, half at a time, blending well to make a stiff dough.

3 Roll dough, a rounded teaspoonful at a time, into balls between palms of hands; place, 1 inch apart, on lightly greased large cookie sheets.

4 Bake in moderate oven (350°) 12 minutes, or until firm. Remove from cookie sheets to wire racks; let cool completely.

5 When ready to frost cookies, place about an inch apart on wire racks set on wax paper or foil. Spoon PEPPERMINT GLAZE over cookies to cover completely; let set slightly. Scrape any frosting that drips onto paper back into bowl; stir well. Spoon another layer over cookies to make a thick coating; let stand until firm. Trim with holly leaves and berries, using decorating frostings in pressurized cans or plastic tubes, if you wish.

PEPPERMINT GLAZE

Combine 3 cups sifted 10X (confectioners' powdered) sugar, 3 tablespoons water, ¼ teaspoon peppermint extract, and ¼ teaspoon red food coloring in a medium-size bowl; beat until smooth. (Frosting will be thin enough to pour from a spoon. If it gets too thick while frosting cookies, add a few drops water and beat again until smooth.) Makes about 1 cup.

Candy Canes

This is a basic recipe—change the food coloring and you change the holiday mood

Bake at 350° for 12 minutes.
Makes 2½ dozen

      2 cups sifted all-purpose flour
    ½ teaspoon baking soda
    ¼ teaspoon salt
    ⅔ cup butter or margarine
    ⅔ cup sugar
      1 whole egg
      1 egg yolk
      1 teaspoon vanilla
         ORNAMENTAL FROSTING (see index for recipe page number)
         Red food coloring

1 Sift flour, soda, and salt onto wax paper.

2 Cream butter or margarine with sugar until fluffy-light in a large bowl; beat in egg, egg yolk, and vanilla. Stir in flour mixture, half at a time, blending well to make a stiff dough.

3 Roll out dough, an eighth at a time, on a lightly floured pastry cloth or board with palms of hands to a log about as thick as a pencil.

Cut into 5-inch lengths. Place, 1 inch apart, on lightly greased large cookie sheets. Curve one end of each to resemble a cane.

4 Bake in moderate oven (350°) 12 minutes, or until firm and lightly golden. Remove from cookie sheets to wire racks; cool completely.

5 Frost canes with part of the ORNAMENTAL FROSTING. Stir a few drops red food coloring into remaining frosting to tint deep pink; press through a cake-decorating set onto frosted canes to form stripes. Let stand on wire racks until frosting is firm.

Candy-Stripe Twists

These fun-to-make cookies taste like old-fashioned licorice sticks

Bake at 350° for 10 minutes.
Makes 5 dozen

    3¼ cups sifted all-purpose flour
      4 teaspoons baking powder
      1 teaspoon salt
    ½ cup (1 stick) butter or margarine
    1¼ cups sugar
      1 egg
    ½ teaspoon oil of anise
    ¼ cup milk
         Red food coloring

1 Measure flour, baking powder, and salt into sifter.

2 Cream butter or margarine and sugar until fluffy in large bowl; beat in egg and oil of anise.

3 Sift in dry ingredients, a third at a time, adding alternately with milk; stir until well-blended.

4 Spoon half of dough into a medium-size bowl; blend in a few drops red food coloring to tint pink; leave other half plain.

5 Pinch off about a teaspoonful each of pink and white doughs at a time, and roll each into a pencil-thin strip about 5 inches long on lightly floured pastry cloth or board. Place strips side by side, pressing ends together, then twist into a rope. Place, 1 inch apart, on ungreased cookie sheets.

6 Bake in moderate oven (350°) 10 minutes, or until firm. Remove carefully from cookie sheets; cool on wire racks. Store, with wax paper or transparent wrap between layers, in container with tight-fitting cover.

Lemon Fondant Frosting

It couldn't be easier, for it's the no-cook kind—and a perfect keeper if stored in a covered jar in the refrigerator

Makes about ¾ cup

2 cups 10X (confectioners' powdered) sugar
2 tablespoons water
1½ teaspoon lemon juice
Yellow and green food colorings

1 Mix 10X sugar with water and lemon juice in a medium-size bowl; beat until smooth.
2 Tint lightly with a drop each of yellow and green food colorings. (Frosting will be just thick enough to pour from a spoon. If it gets too thick while frosting cookies, add a drop or two of water and beat again until smooth. If made ahead, remove from refrigerator about an hour before frosting cookies to soften.)

Pfeffernuss Drops

These sugar dainties have all the spicy flavor of the old-fashioned German kind

Bake at 350° for 8 minutes.
Makes about 6 dozen

1¾ cups sifted all-purpose flour
1 teaspoon ground cinnamon
¼ teaspoon baking soda
¼ teaspoon salt
¼ teaspoon ground nutmeg
⅛ teaspoon ground cloves
⅛ teaspoon pepper
½ teaspoon anise seeds
½ teaspoon crushed cardamom seeds (from 10 pods)
¼ cup candied citron, finely chopped
¼ cup candied orange peel, finely chopped
2 tablespoons butter or margarine
1¼ cups sifted 10X (confectioners' powdered) sugar
1 egg
Red and green candied cherries
1 teaspoon milk

1 Sift first seven ingredients into large bowl; stir in anise seeds, cardamom seeds, citron, and orange peel.
2 Cream butter or margarine and 1 cup 10X sugar until well-mixed in medium-size bowl. (Save remaining ¼ cup for Step 4.) Gradually stir in egg, then flour mixture, just until blended. Chill overnight, or until firm enough to handle.

3 Roll dough, about 1 teaspoonful at a time, into small balls; place, 2 inches apart, on greased cookie sheets. Top each with a piece of candied cherry.
4 Stir milk into saved ¼ cup 10X sugar until smooth in small cup. Drizzle very lightly over top of each cooky.
5 Bake in moderate oven (350°) 8 minutes, or until very lightly browned. Remove from cookie sheets at once; cool on wire racks.

Viennese Rounds

Double-deck cookies with raspberry filling inspired by the famous Linzer torte

Bake at 350° for 10 minutes.
Makes about 3 dozen double cookies

1 cup (2 sticks) butter or margarine
1½ cups sifted 10X (confectioners' powdered) sugar
1½ cups sifted all-purpose flour
1 teaspoon vanilla
½ cup filberts or hazelnuts, ground
Red food coloring
1 cup red raspberry preserves

1 Cream butter or margarine and ½ cup of the 10X sugar until well-blended in a large bowl; stir in flour, vanilla, and ground nuts.
2 Roll dough, a level teaspoonful at a time, into balls between palms of hands. Place, 2 inches apart, on greased cookie sheets. Lightly grease the bottom of a measuring cup and dip in 10X sugar; press over each ball to flatten to an about-1-inch round.
3 Bake in moderate oven (350°) 10 minutes, or until golden around edges. Remove carefully from cookie sheets to wire racks; cool completely.
4 Beat remaining 1 cup 10X sugar with a few drops water until smooth in a small bowl; tint pink with a drop or two food coloring.
5 Spread bottoms of half of the cookies with raspberry preserves; top, sandwich style, with remaining cookies, flat side down.
6 Attach a writing tip to a cake-decorating set; fill decorator with pink frosting; press out in rings on tops of cookies.

Sweet-Tooth Candies For Everyone

Remember gazing at a plate of sugarplum candies and wondering what the buttery fondant stuffing tasted like? Or, looking at the many-colored candy canes hanging on the Christmas tree, and wanting to taste one?

Let your family have memories, too, by cooking these candies in your own kitchen.

FUDGE, FONDANT, AND PENUCHE

Easy No-Beat Fudge

Super smooth and velvety, this is easiest to make if candy thermometer is used

Makes about 3 pounds.

2 packages (6 ounces each) semi-sweet chocolate pieces
3 cups miniature marshmallows
½ cup chopped walnuts
2 cups sugar
⅔ cup (1 small can) evaporated milk
3 tablespoons butter or margarine

1 Butter an 8x8x2-inch pan. Have chocolate, marshmallows and nuts ready.
2 Combine sugar, milk and butter in a heavy medium-size saucepan. Bring to boiling; lower heat. Gently simmer, stirring constantly with wooden spoon to prevent scorching, about 6 minutes, or to 227° on candy thermometer.
3 Remove from heat. Immediately stir in chocolate and marshmallows until melted. Quickly stir in nuts. Spoon into prepared pan; smooth top.

Candies for all occasions: **Candied Popcorn Wreaths** (on tree), **Popcorn-Almond Brittle** (top, left), **Cherry Vanilla Fudge** (left), **Old-Fashioned Chocolate Fudge** (left), **Butterscotch Drops** (center), **Chocolate Truffles** (bottom, center), **Sugarplums** (top, right), and **Candy Canes.**

Allow to firm up, about 30 minutes. Cut into squares. Store in tightly covered container. Refrigerate if kitchen is too warm. Fudge will be softer than classic beaten fudge.

Caramel-Pecan Fudge Rounds

Shape this buttery-rich chocolate confection into rolls to slice as needed

Makes about 2½ pounds

2 cups sugar
⅛ teaspoon salt
2 squares unsweetened chocolate
1 small can evaporated milk (⅔ cup)
2 tablespoons light corn syrup
2 tablespoons butter or margarine
1 teaspoon vanilla
1 package (14 ounces) caramels
1 tablespoon water
2 cups coarsely broken pecans

1 Combine sugar, salt, chocolate, evaporated milk, and corn syrup in a large heavy saucepan.
2 Heat, stirring constantly, just until sugar dissolves and chocolate melts, then cook rapidly, without stirring, to 236° on a candy thermometer. (A teaspoonful of syrup will form a soft ball when dropped in cold water.) Remove from heat.
3 Add butter or margarine and vanilla. (Do not stir in.) Let cool in pan on a wire rack to 110°, or until bottom of pan feels lukewarm.
4 Beat 2 to 3 minutes, or just until fudge starts to thicken and lose its glossiness; pour onto a buttered platter. Let stand 2 to 3 minutes, or just until set and cool enough to handle.
5 Pick up fudge, about half at a time, in your hands and knead until soft. Shape each half into two rolls about 1 inch in diameter and 6 inches long. Place on wax paper.
6 Unwrap caramels and combine with water in the top of a double boiler; heat over hot water, stirring several times, until melted and mixture is creamy-smooth; cool slightly.
7 Spread pecans on a large sheet of wax paper. Working with one fudge roll at a time, spread
(continued)

about half lengthwise with caramel mixture; roll in pecans to coat well. Turn roll; spread remaining with caramel mixture; roll in pecans. Repeat with remaining fudge rolls. Let stand until coating is firm.

8 Wrap rolls tightly in wax paper, foil, or transparent wrap. Store in refrigerator. When ready to serve, slice about ½ inch thick.

Hot Fudge Sauce

The real fudgy kind that stiffens when it's poured on cold ice cream

Makes about 2 cups.

4 squares unsweetened chocolate
2 tablespoons butter or margarine
¾ cup boiling water
2 cups sugar
3 tablespoons corn syrup
2 teaspoons vanilla

1 Coarsely chop chocolate; heat with butter and boiling water in a large heavy saucepan over low heat, stirring constantly until chocolate is melted. Add sugar and corn syrup.

2 Bring mixture slowly to boiling; lower heat; *simmer gently* 7 to 8 minutes. Watch carefully, but do not stir. Test on ice cream or an ice cube, until it firms up as you like it. Add vanilla. Serve while warm. Refrigerate any leftover sauce in screw-top jar.

3 To reheat: Remove cover from jar. Put jar in saucepan of water. Heat, stirring occasionally, until sauce is softened enough to pour. This sauce is great on French Chocolate Ice Cream, pound cake, ice cream filled meringue shells or over banana splits.

Peanut Butter Fudge

Creamy and divinely peanutty—a treat for the whole family

Makes about 2 pounds.

2 cups sugar
½ cup light corn syrup
½ cup milk
¼ teaspoon salt
2 tablespoons butter or margarine
1 teaspoon vanilla
1 cup crunchy or smooth peanut butter
½ cup finely chopped peanuts (optional)

1 Combine sugar, corn syrup, milk and salt in a medium-size saucepan. Cook over *low* heat, stirring constantly, until sugar dissolves. Cover pan for 1 minute to allow the steam to wash down the sugar crystals that cling to side of pan, or wipe down the crystals with a damp cloth.

2 Uncover pan; insert candy thermometer. Cook without stirring until candy thermometer reaches 236° (soft ball stage, where syrup when dropped into very cold water forms a soft ball that flattens on removal from water).

3 Remove from heat. Add butter. Cool syrup until luke-warm (110°). Add vanilla, peanut butter and nuts. Beat until candy begins to thicken and loses its high gloss. Turn immediately into a buttered 8x8x2-inch pan. Score with a sharp knife into small squares; cool. When completely cool, cut squares all the way through. Store 2 to 3 weeks in tightly covered container with foil or plastic wrap between layers.

Cherry Vanilla Fudge

This vanilla fudge is full of bright bits of candied cherries

Makes 1¾ pounds.

3 cups sugar
½ teaspoon salt
1 cup light cream
½ cup milk
¼ cup light corn syrup
2 tablespoons butter or margarine
2 teaspoons vanilla
1 cup red and green candied cherries, cut in quarters

1 Combine sugar, salt, cream, milk, corn syrup and butter in a large heavy saucepan.

2 Cook over medium heat, stirring constantly, until mixture comes to boiling. Continue cooking, stirring occasionally, until candy thermometer reaches 238°. (A teaspoon of the mixture will form a soft ball when dropped into cold water.)

3 Remove from heat, leaving thermometer in the saucepan. Cool to 100°.

4 Add vanilla. Beat briskly until fudge thickens and begins to lose its gloss. Stir in cherries.

5 Pour into buttered 8-inch square pan. Cool. Cut into squares when firm.

TEMPERATURES AND TESTS FOR CANDY

Type of Candy	Temperature on Candy Thermometer (at Sea Level) Degrees F.	Test	Description of Test
Sugar Syrup	230 to 234	Thread	Syrup spins a 2-inch thread when dropped from fork or spoon.
Fondant, Fudge	234 to 240	Soft Ball	Syrup, when dropped into very cold water, forms a soft ball that flattens on removal from water.
Caramels	244 to 248	Firm Ball	Syrup, when dropped into very cold water, forms a firm ball that does not flatten on removal from water.
Divinity, Marshmallows	250 to 266	Hard ball	Syrup, when dropped into very cold water, forms a ball that is hard enough to hold its shape, yet still plastic.
Taffy	270 to 290	Soft Crack	Syrup, when dropped into very cold water, separates into threads that are hard but not brittle.
Brittle, Glacé	300 to 310	Hard Crack	Syrup, when dropped into very cold water, separates into threads that are hard and brittle.

Fabulous Fudge

To be a topnotch fudge maker, it pays to invest in a candy thermometer to eliminate guesswork. The rest is easy—just follow mixing-cooking directions

Makes about 1¼ pounds

2 cups sugar
⅛ teaspoon salt
2 squares unsweetened chocolate
1 small can evaporated milk (⅔ cup)
2 tablespoons white corn syrup
2 tablespoons butter or margarine
½ teaspoon vanilla

1 Combine sugar, salt, chocolate, evaporated milk, and corn syrup in a heavy saucepan. Heat, stirring constantly, just until the sugar dissolves and chocolate melts. Remove spoon; put thermometer in.

2 Cook rapidly, without stirring, to 236°, remove from heat. Add butter or margarine and vanilla (no stirring yet), then let cool on a wire rack to 110°. Bottom of the pan should feel lukewarm.

3 Beat 2 to 3 minutes, or until fudge starts to thicken and lose its glossiness; pour into buttered dish, 10x6x2. Let stand until set—only 2 to 3 minutes; cut at once in smooth neat squares.

Creamy Cocoa Fudge

Candy fans love this old-fashioned treat

Makes 1¼ pounds

⅓ cup dry cocoa (not a mix)
2 cups sugar
  Dash of salt
⅔ cup water
2 tablespoons butter or margarine
1 teaspoon vanilla

1 Combine cocoa, sugar, salt, water, and butter or margarine in a medium-size saucepan. Heat slowly, stirring constantly, to boiling, then cook, without stirring, to 236° on a candy thermometer. (A teaspoon of syrup dropped into cold water will form a soft ball.) Remove from heat; stir in vanilla.
2 Set pan aside on kitchen counter (not in refrigerator) and let cool, *without stirring,* to 110° on candy thermometer. (Bottom of pan should feel lukewarm.)
3 Beat mixture 2 to 3 minutes, or just until it starts to thicken and loses its glossiness.
4 Spoon at once, into 10 one-ounce paper cups or souffle cups or into a buttered loaf pan, 7½x3¾x2¼. (Candy will be about 1-inch deep in loaf pan.)
5 Let stand at room temperature until firm.

Old-Fashioned Chocolate Fudge

Most mothers will remember making a batch of fudge like this in the college dorm to help them get through exams

Makes about 2 pounds.

1½ cups milk
4 squares unsweetened chocolate (4 ounces)
4 cups sugar
3 tablespoons light corn syrup
¼ teaspoon salt
3 tablespoons butter or margarine
1½ teaspoons vanilla

1 Combine milk and chocolate in medium-size heavy saucepan; cook over low heat until chocolate is melted. Add sugar, corn syrup and salt and cook, stirring constantly, to boiling.
2 Cook without stirring to 234° on a candy thermometer. (A teaspoonful of syrup will form a soft ball when dropped in cold water.) Remove from heat at once. Add vanilla and butter or margarine, but do not stir in.
3 Cool mixture in pan to 110°, or until luke-

warm; beat with wooden spoon until mixture thickens and begins to lose its gloss. (This will take about 15 minutes.)
4 Spread in a buttered 8x8x2-inch pan. Let stand until set and cool; cut into squares.

Fast and Smooth Fudge

Here is a quick version of the standard fudge—creamy and delicious, but no beating needed

Makes about 3 pounds.

1⅓ cups sugar
⅔ cup evaporated milk (1 small can)
3 tablespoons butter or margarine
3 packages (6 ounces each) semi-sweet chocolate pieces
3 cups miniature marshmallows
½ cup chopped walnuts
½ cup candied cherries, halved

1 Combine sugar, milk and butter or margarine in a medium-size heavy saucepan; heat to boiling over medium heat, stirring constantly; cook for 6 minutes, or until candy thermometer reaches 227°.
2 Remove from heat; add chocolate pieces and marshmallows; stir until chocolate and marshmallows are melted and mixture is smooth; quickly stir in walnuts and cherries.
3 Spoon into buttered 8x8x2-inch pan; let stand until set; cut into squares. You may press this fudge into tiny tart pans, then decorate with nuts.

Chocolate Truffle Fudge

Chocolate and walnuts combine in this family favorite

Makes about 2 pounds

1 can (14 ounces) sweetened condensed milk
2 packages (12 ounces each) semisweet-chocolate pieces
  Pinch of salt
2 teaspoons vanilla
1 cup finely chopped walnuts

1 Combine sweetened condensed milk, semi-sweet-chocolate pieces, and salt in top of double boiler; heat over simmering water, stirring often, 10 to 12 minutes, or until chocolate is melted. Remove from heat; stir in vanilla, then fold in ¾ cup walnuts.

2 Spread evenly in a buttered 8-inch foil pie plate or in a wax-paper-lined pan, 8x8x2. Sprinkle remaining ¼ cup walnuts over, pressing into fudge. Chill 3 hours, or until firm.

Golden Fudge

So satiny-smooth and creamy it literally melts in your mouth

Makes about 1½ pounds

3 cups sugar
¼ cup light corn syrup
3 tablespoons butter or margarine
½ teaspoon salt
1 cup evaporated milk
½ cup water
2 teaspoons vanilla
Green and red candied cherries

1 Combine sugar, corn syrup, butter or margarine, salt, evaporated milk, and water in a medium-size heavy saucepan.

2 Heat, stirring constantly, to boiling, then cook rapidly, stirring several times, to 238° on a candy thermometer. (A teaspoonful of syrup will form a soft ball when dropped in cold water.) Remove from heat at once. Add vanilla, but do not stir in.

3 Cool mixture in pan to 110°, or until lukewarm; beat 2 to 3 minutes, or until it starts to thicken and lose its gloss.

4 Spread in a buttered pan, 8x8x2. Let stand 2 to 3 minutes, or just until set; cut into squares. Decorate each with slivered cherries. Let stand until firm.

Basic White Fondant

Use this basic recipe for a candy, or the filling of a candy

Makes about 1½ pounds

3 cups sifted granulated sugar
1 cup hot water
1 tablespoon white corn syrup
   OR: ⅛ teaspoon cream of tartar

1 Combine ingredients; cook together until candy thermometer reads 238°-242°.

2 Pour mixture onto marble slab or stainless steel pan until it cools to 110°.

3 Work syrup until it is thick, white, and creamy. Cool, then shape into balls for dipping in melted chocolate or knead in a few drops red, yellow or green food coloring and shape in fondant molds.

Sugarplums

Rich little morsels with a sweet stuffing of buttery fondant

Makes 2 pounds.

½ pound dried apricots
½ pound dried pitted prunes
½ pound dried figs
3 cups sugar
2 cups water
¼ teaspoon cream of tartar
2 tablespoons butter or margarine
   Sugar

1 Place dried fruits in a strainer and steam over boiling water until plump and soft (about 10-15 minutes). Cover with foil until ready to stuff.

2 Make fondant stuffing: Combine sugar, water and cream of tartar in a deep heavy saucepan. Stir until sugar is completely dissolved. Then cover the saucepan and cook for 3 minutes. Uncover. Insert candy thermometer into mixture. Do not stir. Continue cooking until the thermometer reads exactly 239°.

3 Pour syrup on a piece of marble, a large china platter, or other smooth surface.

4 Let mixture stand 30 minutes, until it begins to set. (The mixture will be clear in appearance, while later it will appear as thick white icing.

5 With a wide spatula, scrape the mixture up from one side and smooth it back to the area from which it was scraped. Work from each side towards the opposite side, keeping the mixture in motion as you move it to and fro. It will begin to thicken and turn white, and suddenly it will turn into a firm mass. Begin to knead this dough-like mixture immediately for 5 minutes, or until very smooth.

6 While one person kneads the fondant, have a second person cut the butter into bits, and knead into the fondant, until evenly distributed throughout.

7 Dust your hands lightly with cornstarch or flour, and roll the fondant into ½-inch balls.

8 Stuff each piece of steamed fruit with a fondant ball, pressing fruit around fondant.

(continued)

9 Roll stuffed fruit in sugar to coat liberally. Wrap in squares of plastic wrap, twisting ends to make airtight and to keep soft.
Note: Fondant may be made in advance and placed in tightly covered crock or jar for two or three days before using.

Creamy Penuche

This member of the fudge family might have been the very one grandma cooked up to serve her best beau

Makes about 2 pounds.

2 cups firmly packed light brown sugar
1 cup granulated sugar
¼ cup dark corn syrup
2 tablespoons butter or margarine
¾ cup milk
⅛ teaspoon salt
1 teaspoon vanilla

1 Combine sugars, corn syrup, butter or margarine, milk and salt in a medium-size heavy saucepan.
2 Heat, stirring constantly, to boiling, then cook, stirring several times, to 238° on a candy thermometer. (A teapoonful of syrup will form a soft ball when dropped in cold water.) Remove from heat at once. Add vanilla, but do not stir in.
3 Cool mixture in pan to 110°, or until lukewarm; beat with wooden spoon until mixture thickens and begins to lose its gloss. (This will take about 15 minutes.)
4 Spread in buttered 9x5x3-inch loaf pan. Let stand until set and cool; cut into squares.

Frosted Penuche Squares

Like penuche and divinity? They're doubly good when combined in one treat

Makes 2 pounds

BASIC PENUCHE
2 cups firmly packed brown sugar
1½ cups granulated sugar
3 tablespoons butter or margarine
¼ teaspoon salt
1½ cups milk

BASIC DIVINITY
2 cups sugar
½ cup light corn syrup
½ cup water
2 egg whites
1 teaspoon vanilla
½ cup chopped pistachio nuts

1 Make Basic Penuche: Combine brown and granulated sugars, butter or margarine, salt, and milk in a large heavy saucepan.
2 Heat, stirring constantly, just until sugar dissolves, then cook rapidly, without stirring, to 240° on a candy thermometer. (A teaspoonful of syrup will form a soft ball when dropped into cold water.) Remove from heat.
3 Cool in pan on a wire rack to 110°, or until bottom of pan feels lukewarm.
4 Beat 8 to 10 minutes, or until mixture is light in color and very thick. (It will still be glossy.) Pour into a buttered pan, 8x8x2; cool.
5 Make Basic Divinity: Combine sugar, corn syrup, and water in a medium-size heavy saucepan. Heat, stirring constantly, to boiling. (Have a fork wrapped in a piece of damp cheesecloth handy and wipe off any sugar crystals that form on side of pan as mixture heats.)
6 Cook rapidly, without stirring, to 260° on a candy thermometer. (A teaspoonful of syrup will form a hard ball when dropped in cold water.) Remove from heat.
7 While syrup cooks, beat egg whites until they stand in firm peaks in a medium-size bowl. *Beating constantly,* pour in syrup in a fine stream; beat in vanilla, then continue beating until mixture is very stiff and holds its shape. Spread over butterscotch layer in pan. Sprinkle with pistachio nuts.
8 Let stand until firm. Cut in small squares.

Divinity-Nut Puffs

These wisps of creamy candy are a delight at holidaytime. One batch makes two kinds

Makes about 1½ pounds

2 cups sugar
½ cup light corn syrup
½ cup water
2 egg whites
½ teaspoon lemon extract
½ teaspoon almond extract

Few drops green food coloring
24 *blanched almonds (from an about-5-ounce
    can)*
 2 *tablespoons chopped pistachio nuts*

1 Combine sugar, corn syrup, and water in a medium-size saucepan; heat, stirring several times, to boiling. (Have a fork wrapped in a piece of damp cheesecloth handy and wipe off any sugar crystals that form on side of pan as mixture heats.)
2 Cook rapidly, without stirring, to 240° on a candy thermometer. (A teaspoon of syrup dropped into cold water will form a soft ball that flattens very slightly.)
3 While syrup cooks, beat egg whites until they stand in firm peaks in the medium-size bowl of an electric mixer. Beating constantly, pour ⅓ of the syrup over egg whites in a fine stream to form a meringue.
4 Cook remaining syrup rapidly to 265° on candy thermometer. (A teaspoon of syrup dropped into cold water will form a ball that is hard enough to hold its shape.)
5 Pour, still beating constantly, in a fine stream over meringue mixture; continue beating until mixture is very stiff and holds its shape.
6 Divide into two bowls. Stir lemon extract into one bowl and almond extract and several drops green food coloring into second bowl.
7 Drop by teaspoonfuls into small mounds on wax-paper-lined or foil-lined cooky sheets. Top each white mound with an almond (toast first, if you wish); sprinkle each green mound with pistachio nuts. (If candy turns too stiff while shaping mounds, beat in one or two *drops* hot water.) Let stand until firm.

Note: Choose a clear dry day to make this candy. When air is damp or humid, meringue mixture may pick up moisture, causing puffs to flatten and become sticky. Make not more than three or four days ahead, then store between layers of wax paper, foil, or transparent wrap in a container with a tight-fitting cover to keep out moisture.

The family won't mind dipping its hands into these delicious **Divinity-Nut Puffs.**

CANDY BASICS:

SUGAR

Granulated. Take your pick of cane or beet sugars, in bag or box, for both are excellent and our cheapest energy food. Watch for specials on 5- or 10-pound bags, for they are the thriftiest buys of all. Other products in this class are super-fine or very fine sugar, often called for in special cake, pudding, and candy recipes; tablets and cubes in various sizes and shapes in 1-, 1½-, and 2-pound cartons; cinnamon-sugar, ready to sprinkle right from the jar on breakfast toast or a fruit dessert; and a variety of colored sugars for decorating cookies, cakes, and candies. Compared to granulated sugar, all of the specialty items cost more, but are often worth it in convenience.

10X. Also known as confectioners' or confectioners' powdered, this is our popular frosting sugar and is labeled both 10X and 4X. The X's simply mean a slight difference in texture, with 10X being the finer of the two.

Brown. This favorite owes its color and flavor to the small amount of molasses that clings to the sugar crystals during processing. You'll find it labeled LIGHT, MEDIUM, or DARK BROWN, in 1-pound cartons, or, in some areas, in 2-pound transparent bags. Which you choose depends on your flavor preference. Consider, too, GRANULATED BROWN SUGAR, packed in 1-pound, 4-ounce cartons. As its name suggests, it pours easily and does not need to be packed before measuring.

HOW DOES SUGAR MEASURE UP?

If you're fixing a special recipe, it pays to know just how much sugar to buy. Here is a pin-up guide for quick reference:

- One pound of granulated sugar measures 2⅓ cups.

- One pound 10X (confectioners' powdered) sugar yields 4 cups if unsifted, or about 4½ cups if sifted.

- One pound light or dark brown sugar firmly packed, measures 2¼ to 2⅓ cups.

- One pound of loaf sugar—120 pieces.

THE WONDERFUL WORLD OF CHOCOLATE CANDY

What would fudge, fondants, and fruit centers be without chocolate? When we think of one, we think of the other. But what type of chocolate to buy, how to melt it for best use, and, very importantly, how to store it, are subjects that beginning chocolate-candy makers often do not understand. Here is a quick let's-get-acquainted survey.

TYPES OF CHOCOLATE

Unsweetened. Often referred to as baking or cooking chocolate, this old-timer in the bar-shape package has a rich bitter flavor that's ideal for brownies, cookies, fudge, cakes, sauces, desserts. Each package, weighing 8 ounces, contains separately wrapped 1-ounce squares.

Liquid unsweetened. Packed in 1-ounce transparent envelopes, this needs no melting or measuring, can be squeezed handily right from the envelope into batter or beverage. Use it in any recipe that calls for unsweetened chocolate or cocoa, 1 envelope for 1 square of chocolate or ¼ cup dry cocoa.

Semi-sweet. It looks like unsweetened bar chocolate and is packaged the same way, but it contains some sugar. It melts smoothly and quickly to stir into frostings, fillings, and candies.

Semi-sweet pieces. Unsweetened chocolate plus cocoa butter, sugar, and a vanilla-type flavoring go into this popular ingredient. Although the tiny nuggets will melt creamy-smooth for candy or sauces, they hold their shape during baking in cakes and cookies. Package sizes: Six and 12 ounces.

Sweet. Also tagged sweet-cooking chocolate, each 4-ounce bar contains 18 small squares of a special blend: Unsweetened chocolate, sugar, cocoa butter, and vanilla. For cakes, pies, frostings, and sauces that need a rich but light flavor, it's an excellent choice. Although not a milk chocolate, it's a delicious stand-in for a candy bar.

Milk chocolate. The popular candy-bar chocolate, made somewhat like sweet chocolate but with cream added to give it a lighter color and milder flavor. Buy it in bars, bulk, or pieces to suit your preference.

Today's candy counters are a happy hunting ground, with their almost unlimited variety of solid milk-chocolate bars, chocolate-coated candy, and dozens of combination bars containing fruits and nuts alone or together. You've probably noticed, too, that many of your favorite recipes call for a chocolate bar to add interesting flavor and crunch. And when it comes to timesavers, most cooks will agree that a melted chocolate bar is a mighty fast way to a frosting.

Cocoa. This breakfast regular is unsweetened chocolate with most of the cocoa butter (fat) removed. "Dutch process" marked on the label simply tells you that the cocoa has been treated to give it a rich dark color and robust flavor. Expect to pay a little bit more for this type than for regular cocoa.

Instant cocoa *mixes,* not to be confused with regular cocoa, are a blend of cocoa, sugar, flavoring, and sometimes nonfat dry milk. Stir them into hot or cold milk or water for an instant pickup. Container sizes vary from 8 ounces to 2 pounds. Reminder: In recipes—for baked foods and candies, especially—*do not substitute instant cocoa mix for cocoa.*

HOW TO MELT CHOCOLATE

Methods are many, but one precaution is a must with them all: Go easy on the heat—chocolate burns and scorches quickly. Unsweetened, semisweet, and sweet may be melted over hot *(not boiling)* water, but guard against moisture or steam, either causes the chocolate to stiffen.

Another trick is to place the chocolate in a greased pie plate in a warm oven until melted. Unsweetened chocolate may also be melted in a heavy saucepan over very low direct heat, but this takes constant watching and stirring. For some recipes, such as candies, double up on steps by melting the chocolate with the butter or margarine, or in the liquid (milk, water, or coffee).

A favorite of many homemakers that's practically effortless: Place the chocolate in a double boiler over water; cover; heat until water bubbles, then turn off the heat. Let stand until chocolate softens; stir until smooth.

HOW TO STORE CHOCOLATE

With chocolate as with most foods, there's a best method of storing. Basically, it should be kept cool—about 75°—and dry. If chocolate gets warmer, the cocoa butter comes to the surface, melts, and forms a grayish white film as it cools. While this doesn't affect the flavor, it does mar the appearance. Sometimes, under the best conditions, this happens anyway. If it does, just melt the chocolate—this restores its color.

Chocolate may also be kept in the refrigerator, provided you wrap it first, then place in a tightly covered container so it won't absorb odors. Keep cocoa in a tightly sealed container in a cool spot (not the refrigerator). Under other conditions it, too, fades and tends to lump.

Butter Cream Centers

Velvety-smooth on the outside, with a creamy inside

Makes about 1½ pounds, enough for 40 candies

    3 cups sugar
    1 cup water
    ¼ teaspoon cream of tartar
    ¼ cup butter
    ¼ teaspoon salt
    1 teaspoon vanilla
    ⅛ teaspoon baking soda in ½ teaspoon hot
        water

1 Cook sugar, water, and cream of tartar to 238°-240° on a candy thermometer. Add baking soda and hot water, mixed, to the combination. **2** Pour onto cool marble or a stainless steel pan. Let stand 5 minutes, or until center feels lukewarm (110-115° on a candy thermometer). **3** Cream 5 minutes; add butter; work like fondant until cool and thick, 10 minutes. Knead 1 minute. Add nuts or other flavorings. Cool, then shape into balls for dipping in melted chocolate.

CANDY BASICS: HOW TO STORE CANDY

Fudge—*Leave candy right in its pan and cover tightly with foil to keep it creamy-soft, then place it in a cool, dry spot. While fudge mellows upon standing, it's a good idea to make it no longer than a week or two ahead of serving or giving.*

Caramels—*To hold these chewy treats at their best, wrap each piece separately in transparent wrap so the candy shows through invitingly, and tuck away in a covered container in your cupboard.*

Uncooked fondant—*For top flavor, this confection should "ripen" for a few days before eating. Bundle the rolls into a plastic bag, seal tightly, and chill to slice as needed. Leaving the rolls whole helps to keep them moist and flavorful.*

Full Cream Caramels

Chocolate-covered candies for the whole family

Makes about 1½ pounds

>   2 cups sugar
>   1 cup light corn syrup
>   1½ cups warm cream for whipping with ½ cup water
>   ¼ cup butter
>   ½ teaspoon salt
>   1 teaspoon vanilla

1 Cook sugar, syrup, 1 cup cream and ¼ cup water for 10 minutes. Add remaining warm cream and remaining water; cook slowly for 5 minutes.
2 Add butter, small amount at a time. When candy thermometer reaches 230°, lower heat; cook slowly to 244-246° on thermometer.
3 Allow to stand 10 minutes. Add salt, vanilla and pour into well-oiled or buttered 18-inch pan. Cool until solid enough to cut, then, if you like, dip into chocolate.

Molasses Coconut Chews

Tender little nuggets bursting with coconut

Makes 2½ pounds with chocolate or 2¼ pounds without.

>   1¼ cups sugar
>   ⅔ cup light corn syrup
>   ⅓ cup molasses
>   2 tablespoons butter or margarine
>   3 cans (4 ounces each) shredded coconut (about 4 cups)

1 Combine sugar, corn syrup, molasses and butter or margarine in a large saucepan. Cook, stirring constantly, until sugar dissolves. Cover pan for 1 minute to allow the steam to wash down the sugar crystals that cling to side of pan; or, wipe down the crystals with a damp cloth.
2 Uncover pan; insert candy thermometer. Cook without stirring until candy thermometer reaches 253° (hard ball stage, where syrup when dropped in very cold water forms a ball in the fingers that is hard enough to hold a shape, yet still plastic).
3 Remove from heat; stir in the coconut. Pour mixture into a well-buttered 13x9x2-inch pan. Cool until lukewarm or comfortable to handle.

4 Form candy into ½-inch balls, then cool completely before coating with granulated sugar or chocolate.

SUGAR COATING
Roll cooled balls in granulated sugar.

FOR CHOCOLATE COATING
Melt 1 large package (12 ounces) semi-sweet chocolate pieces in top of double boiler over hot—not boiling—water. Dip each coconut ball in the chocolate. Lift out with a fork; tap off excess chocolate on edge of pan. Cool on wax paper until chocolate is firm. Store 2 to 3 weeks in refrigerator or in tightly covered container with foil or plastic wrap between layers in a cool dry place.

CANNY WAYS WITH POPCORN

Caramel Popcorn Balls

Make up a batch for your next fund-raising function

Makes ten 4-inch balls

⅔ cup sugar
⅔ cup light corn syrup
½ teaspoon salt
8 cups popped corn
25 caramel candy cubes

1 Combine sugar, corn syrup, and salt in a small saucepan. Heat, stirring, until sugar dissolves.
2 Pour over 8 cups popped corn in a kettle; toss to coat evenly. Cook slowly, stirring, 5 minutes more, or until very sticky.
3 Shape about ¾ cup at a time into a ball; stick a straw into each; repeat to make 10 balls.
4 Melt caramel cubes in double boiler over simmering water; spread with small spatula over top of balls; set on a buttered pan to cool and harden. Wrap in transparent wrap, if you like.

Popcorn Balls

Hang these low on the tree, and let small children untie them at the party

Makes 16 to 24

⅔ cup sugar
⅔ cup light corn syrup

½ teaspoon salt
8 cups popped corn

1 Combine sugar, corn syrup, and salt in a saucepan. Heat, stirring, until sugar dissolves; remove from heat.
2 Pour over 8 cups popped corn in a kettle; toss to coat evenly. Cook slowly, stirring, 5 minutes more, or until very sticky.
3 Shape by heaping tablespoonfuls into balls.

Candied Popcorn Wreaths

You'll certainly have an old-fashioned good time making these candied popcorn wreaths to hang on the tree

Makes 2 dozen (3-inch diameter) wreaths.

4 cups unsalted popcorn
4 cups sugar
1¾ cups light corn syrup
1¼ cups water
8 drops green food coloring
24 red licorice strings

1 Using a large needle, string 6 inches of heavy thread with popcorn. Tie ends to form a 3-inch diameter circle. Repeat, making about 2 dozen popcorn circles. Set aside.
2 Prepare muffin-pan cups to be used in shaping the wreaths by turning the muffin pans upside down and covering the back of each cup with a square of aluminum foil. Place near the range where you will be working, as speed will be important when you dip and shape the wreaths.
3 Stir together in a heavy 3-quart saucepan the sugar, corn syrup, water and green food coloring. Bring to boiling over medium heat, stirring constantly. Then continue cooking, without stirring, until temperature reaches 300° on candy thermometer. (A teaspoon of syrup will separate into hard brittle threads when dropped into cold water.)
4 Turn heat very low, leaving candy thermometer in the saucepan so you can adjust heat if temperature lowers too drastically. Do not let thermometer go over 300°.
5 Then working quickly, dip popcorn wreaths into mixture with 2 forks, one at a time, coating thoroughly. Place wreath on the prepared back of the muffin cup, pressing down slightly to form a round. Continue until all are coated. When all are dipped, spoon remaining syrup over wreaths on muffin cups to coat well. If solid

(continued)

centers are desired, place wreath on a sheet of aluminum foil and spoon extra syrup into center. When almost hardened, poke a small hole near the top of solid center so it can be strung easily.

6 When wreaths harden, pull foil from muffin cups and peel foil from wreath. Break off excess dribbles. Gently wrap in wax paper and store in tightly covered container in a cool place until ready to hang on tree. Tie with red licorice strings, forming a bow at top of each wreath and use an ornament wire to hang.

Note: Any leftover syrup may be spooned onto lollipop sticks placed on aluminum foil. Flavor first with several drops of oil of peppermint, if you wish.

Tutti-Frutti Popcorn Balls

Party nibbles that go well with any soft drink

Makes about 50 small balls

10 cups freshly popped corn
 1 can (6 ounces) pecans
 1 jar (4 ounces) candied red cherries, halved
 1 package (1 pound) 10X (confectioners' powdered) sugar, sifted
⅔ cup light corn syrup
 2 tablespoons water
   Red food coloring
16 large marshmallows (¼ pound)
¾ teaspoon peppermint extract

1 Mix popcorn, pecans, and cherries in two buttered jelly-roll pans.
2 Combine about 1 cup of the 10X sugar, corn syrup, and water in a medium-size saucepan. Heat slowly, stirring constantly, until sugar dissolves; stir in a few drops food coloring to tint light pink.
3 Stir in remaining 10X sugar slowly; heat, stirring constantly, to boiling. Stir in marshmallows until melted; remove from heat. Stir in peppermint extract.
4 Pour half of the syrup over popcorn mixture in each pan; toss until evenly coated. Cool until easy to handle, then shape into 1½-inch balls. Let stand on wax paper until firm. Store in a tightly covered container.

Almond-Popcorn Clusters

Heap them in a bowl, then watch as they disappear fast

Makes about 2½ dozen

⅓ cup sugar
 3 tablespoons molasses
 3 tablespoons dark corn syrup
 1 teaspoon butter or margarine
 1 teaspoon lemon juice
 4 cups freshly popped corn
 1 package (6 ounces) whole unblanched almonds (about 1 cup)
 1 cup salted toasted coconut chips (from a 4-ounce can)

1 Combine sugar, molasses, corn syrup, butter or margarine, and lemon juice in a kettle. Heat slowly, stirring constantly, just until sugar dissolves; remove from heat.
2 Stir in popcorn, almonds, and coconut chips; toss until evenly coated. Cook, stirring constantly, over medium heat, 5 minutes, or until mixture is very sticky.
3 Spoon out onto wax paper. Let stand a few minutes until cool enough to handle, then shape into 2-inch clusters. Let stand until coating is firm and dry. Store in a loosely covered container.

CANDIED FRUIT

Candied Orange Peel

A sure-fire family and friends favorite

Makes about 2 pounds

5 large oranges
2 cups sugar
1 cup water
3 tablespoons light corn syrup
2 packages (3 ounces each) orange-flavor gelatin

1 Cut rind of each orange in quarters with a sharp knife, then peel off. Place in a heavy large saucepan.
2 Pour in cold water to cover; heat to boiling. Simmer 10 minutes; drain. Add fresh water; simmer 5 minutes; drain.

Next time the family is bored, give them a togetherness-project—making candied fruit.

3 Carefully scrape white membrane from rind with the tip of a teaspoon; cut rind into thin even strips.

4 Combine sugar, water, and corn syrup in same saucepan; heat over medium heat, stirring constantly, until sugar dissolves. Stir in orange rind. Cook over medium heat, stirring often from bottom of pan, 30 minutes, or until rind is almost transparent and syrup is absorbed; drain.

5 Sprinkle gelatin in a large shallow pan; roll strips while warm, one at a time, in gelatin to coat generously. Place on wire racks; let stand until dry. Store in a loosely covered container.

Candied Apples

At the July 4th picnic, hang these on the lowest branches of a tree

Makes 8

8 medium-size red apples
8 flat wooden skewers

2 cups sugar
1 cup light corn syrup
½ cup water
¼ cup (1¾-ounce bottle) red cinnamon candies
10 drops red food coloring (optional)

1 Wash and dry apples; remove stems and insert skewers into stem ends.

2 Mix sugar, corn syrup and water in heavy 2-quart saucepan. Cook over medium heat, stirring constantly, until mixture boils and sugar is dissolved. Then cook, without stirring, until temperature reaches 250° or until small amount of syrup dropped into very cold water forms a ball which is hard enough to hold its shape, yet plastic. Add cinnamon candies and continue cooking to 285° or until small amount of syrup dropped into very cold water separates into threads which are hard, but not brittle.

3 Remove from heat. Stir in red food coloring, if desired. Hold each apple by its skewer and quickly twirl in syrup, tilting pan to cover apple with syrup. Remove apple from syrup; allow excess to drip off, then twirl to spread syrup

(continued)

smoothly over apple. Place on lightly greased baking sheet to cool. Store in cool place.

Note: If candy mixture cools too quickly it may be reheated over low heat.

Candied Fruit Peel

This sweet treat is different. Freshly made, it's tangy and soft and stays just that way. Plain gelatin dissolved in the syrupy coating is the secret. Because it's such a good keeper, it can be made up early for gifts, family snacks, or a garnish for holiday fruit salads and desserts.

Makes 1½ pounds

Peel from 3 oranges
Peel from 1 grapefruit
2½ cups sugar
1 tablespoon light corn syrup
1 teaspoon ground ginger
⅛ teaspoon salt
1½ cups water
1 envelope unflavored gelatin

Follow these easy steps:
1 Peel rind from fruits in quarters; trim off white membrane, then cut rind into ¼-inch-wide strips. Place in large saucepan with water to cover; heat to boiling; simmer 15 minutes. Drain; repeat cooking with fresh water and draining two more times. Return rind to pan.
2 Stir in 2 cups of the sugar, corn syrup, ginger, salt, and 1 cup of the water. Cook slowly, stirring often from bottom of pan, 40 minutes, or until most of syrup is absorbed. Have the gelatin softened in remaining ½ cup water ready; stir it in until dissolved, then cool.
3 Lift out strips, one at a time, and roll in remaining ½ cup sugar, sprinkled on a sheet of wax paper, to coat generously. Place in a single layer on a cooky sheet to dry slightly. If stored in a tightly covered container, peel will keep fragrantly moist for weeks.

CHEWY CARAMELS

Choco-Caramel Top Hats

Almost like magic, packaged caramels turn into the richest sweet-tooth tempter

Makes about 2 pounds

1 package (14 ounces) caramels
¼ cup cream for whipping
1 can (8 ounces) walnuts (2 cups)
6 squares semisweet chocolate

1 Unwrap caramels and combine with cream in the top of a medium-size double boiler. Heat over simmering water about an hour; stir until creamy-smooth. Break walnuts coarsely and stir in.
2 Drop by teaspoonfuls, 1 inch apart, on buttered cooky sheets. Let stand at least an hour, or until firm.
3 While caramel mixture cools, wash top of double boiler, then heat semisweet chocolate over hot water until partly melted; remove from heat; stir until completely melted.
4 Drop, ¼ teaspoonful for each, onto top of caramels; spread slightly. Let stand until firm.

Pecan Nut Caramels

Such a lovely chewy candy, so buttery and delicious!

Makes 2 pounds.

¾ cup finely chopped pecans
2 cups sugar
½ cup (1 stick) butter or margarine
¾ cup light corn syrup
2 cups evaporated milk (from 2 tall cans)

1 Butter an 8x8x2-inch pan; sprinkle evenly with half the chopped pecans.
2 Combine sugar, butter or margarine and corn syrup in a medium-size heavy saucepan. Stir in 1 cup of the evaporated milk. Bring to boiling over medium heat, stirring constantly.
3 Add remaining evaporated milk slowly so that mixture continues to boil. Cook, stirring constantly, over medium heat until candy thermometer registers 244°. (A teaspoonful of syrup will form a firm ball when dropped in cold water.) This will take about 40 minutes.
4 Pour hot caramel immediately into prepared pan. Sprinkle top with remaining chopped pecans. Cool; cut into squares.

CANDY BASICS:

SYRUPS

Corn and Cane. *Their names identify their source, and there are both light and dark kinds. Some are a pure syrup; others have sugar and flavoring added.*

Blended. *Look around, for there's a choice to suit every taste, and true to their name, they are a blend of several pure syrups. Those labeled pancake or waffle syrup combine corn and cane syrups; butter-blended has butter added; and flavored syrups mix maple, fruit, or honey flavors with the syrup. Babies of the family are fruit-juice syrups that are cooked with sugar to pour over pancakes or desserts.*

Maple. *Famous for its delicate flavor, it comes from the sap of the maple tree. And since it takes about 45 gallons of sap to produce a gallon of pure syrup, it carries a de luxe price tag. Other items to con-sider are maple-sugar syrup, maple-blended syrup, and flavored maple syrup.*

Honey. *The flavor and color depend upon the kinds of flowers from which the bees gather nectar. Most usual: Clover or alfalfa. Color is your best guide to flavor, for light honey is mild, while dark tastes stronger. Along with liquid honey in glass jars, pails, and squeeze tubes, you'll find comb honey in 4-inch-square wooden frames, chunk or bulk honey, and granulated or crystalline honey, often labeled* CREAMED.

Molasses. *Depending on how it is made, it may be either sulphured or unsulphured, but both are equally good. Blackstrap molasses, a result of the final boiling in sugar-making, has a black color and strong flavor. Although sometimes promoted as a health food, it has the same food value as regular molasses.*

Caramel Divinity Roll

Fluffy and fruit-filled, this old-fashioned favorite is dressed up in a coating of chewy caramel and crunchy nuts

Makes 2½ pounds or about 5 dozen slices.

2 cups sugar
½ cup light corn syrup
½ cup water
2 egg whites
¼ teaspoon salt
½ cup finely chopped red and green candied cherries
1 package (14 ounces) caramels
1 tablespoon water
1 can (6 ounces) pecans, chopped

1 Combine sugar, corn syrup and water in a medium-size heavy saucepan. Heat quickly to boiling, stirring constantly. Wrap a fork with damp paper towels; wipe the sugar crystals from the side of the pan as the mixture cooks.
2 Reduce heat to medium; cook, without stirring, to 260° on a candy thermometer. (A teaspoonful of syrup will form a hard ball when dropped in cold water.)
3 When syrup reaches 250°, beat egg whites and salt until they stand in firm peaks in a large bowl of electric mixer. *Beating constantly,* pour hot syrup *very slowly* into egg whites. (If you don't have a standard mixer, have someone in the family beat, while you pour.) Continue beating until mixture is very stiff, and will hold marks of beater in mixture (about 7 minutes.)
4 Stir in candied fruits until well distributed. Turn out mixture onto a buttered cookie sheet; divide in half; shape each half into a roll 2 inches wide and 8 inches long. Allow to dry on cookie sheet about one hour.
5 Melt caramels with remaining water in the top of a double boiler, over hot water, stirring several times.
6 Spread pecans on a large sheet of wax paper, working with one roll at a time, spread with caramel mixture; roll in pecans to coat well.
7 Wrap each roll in foil or plastic; store at room temperature. Cut into ¼-inch thick slices.

Pralines

Buttery-rich and packed with pecans, this version boasts a quick-fix trick

Makes about 2 pounds

1 package (3 ounces) vanilla-flavor pudding and pie filling mix
1½ cups firmly packed light brown sugar
½ cup evaporated milk
1 tablespoon butter or margarine
2 cups pecan halves

1 Combine pudding mix, brown sugar, evaporated milk, and butter or margarine in a medium-size heavy saucepan. Heat slowly, stirring constantly, until sugar dissolves, then cook, without stirring, to 238° on a candy thermometer. (A teaspoonful of syrup will form a soft ball when dropped in cold water.) Remove from heat at once.
2 Stir in pecans, then beat with a wooden spoon 2 to 3 minutes, or until mixture starts to thicken.
3 Drop by tablespoonfuls, 2 inches apart, on wax paper. (If mixture hardens as you work, set pan over hot water.) Let stand until firm.

Fruit Caramels

Good keepers and travelers, they're an ideal choice for a gift box

Makes about 2½ pounds

¾ cup golden raisins
¼ cup dried apricot halves
1¼ cups firmly packed brown sugar
1¼ cups light corn syrup
1⅔ cups light cream or table cream
¾ teaspoon salt
1½ teaspoons rum flavoring or extract

1 Chop raisins and apricot halves very fine. Set aside for Step 3.
2 Combine brown sugar, corn syrup, cream, and salt in a medium-size heavy saucepan. Heat slowly, stirring constantly, to boiling, then cook rapidly, stirring constantly, to 246° on a candy thermometer. (A teaspoonful of syrup will form a firm ball when dropped in cold water.) Remove from heat at once.
3 Stir in chopped fruits and rum flavoring or extract. Pour into a buttered pan, 8x8x2. Chill just until firm.
4 Loosen candy around edges with a knife; invert onto a cutting board; cut into 1-inch squares.

TAFFY AND CANDY CANES

Vanilla Taffy

Taffy pulls were a great favorite for young folks' gatherings on winter evenings

Makes ½ pound.

1 cup sugar
⅔ cup light corn syrup
½ cup water
¼ teaspoon cream of tartar
1 teaspoon vanilla
1 tablespoon butter or margarine

1 Butter a large platter or jelly-roll pan.
2 Combine sugar, corn syrup, water and cream of tartar in medium-size heavy saucepan. Bring to boiling over medium heat, stirring constantly.
3 Boil mixture without stirring until candy thermometer registers 266°. (A teaspoonful of syrup will form a hard ball when dropped in cold water.) Remove from heat; stir in vanilla and butter or margarine.
4 Pour onto prepared platter or jelly-roll pan. Let candy stand until cool enough to handle.
5 Butter hands. Gather up candy; pull between hands until it becomes satiny and light in color. Pull into long strips; twist. Cut into 1-inch pieces with scissors. To store, wrap each candy in plastic wrap and place in air-tight container.

Molasses Taffy

Ask your young cooks to join you in an old-fashioned taffy pull

Makes about 1½ pounds

2 cups sugar
3 tablespoons butter or margarine
¼ teaspoon salt
½ cup molasses
½ cup water
2 teaspoons cider vinegar

1 Combine all ingredients in a large heavy saucepan.
2 Heat, stirring constantly, until sugar dissolves, then cook rapidly, without stirring, to 265° on a candy thermometer. (A teaspoonful of syrup will form a hard ball when dropped in cold water.) Remove from heat. *(continued)*

Vary the candy and you vary the pleasure. And what a table of beauties are here—(from the top, clockwise) **Butterscotch Patties, Peanut Brittle, Orange and Lemon Drops, Caramel Divinity Roll, Pecan Nut Caramels,** and **Vanilla Taffy** (see index for recipes).

3 Pour onto a buttered large platter; cool until easy to handle.

4 Butter hands generously. Pick up candy, half at a time, and pull back and forth until golden and candy holds its shape. (Tip: While working with part of the candy, place remaining in a barely warm oven [200°] to keep soft.) Twist each half into a rope about 1 inch in diameter. Snip into 1-inch lengths with scissors. Let stand on waxed paper until firm.

5 Wrap each piece in wax paper, foil, or transparent wrap, twisting ends to seal. Store in a cool, dry place.

Candy Canes

Old-fashioned taffy is twisted like a barber pole, and then cut and looped into candy canes

Makes about 1 pound.

2 cups sugar
1½ cups light corn syrup
1 cup water
½ teaspoon peppermint extract
¼ teaspoon red food coloring

1 Combine sugar, corn syrup and water in heavy saucepan. Bring to boiling over medium heat, stirring constantly, until sugar dissolves. Continue cooking, without stirring, to 260° on a candy thermometer. (A teaspoonful of syrup will form a hard ball when dropped into cold water.)

2 Remove from heat. Quickly stir in peppermint extract.

3 Pour one half of the mixture into a buttered 8-inch square pan.

4 Quickly add red coloring to the remaining mixture and pour into another buttered 8-inch square pan.

5 When cool enough to handle, pull each pan of taffy separately until it has a satin-like finish and light color. (To pull taffy, butter hands and stretch the taffy with a partner, being careful not to twist the taffy and lose the air that causes porousness. If working alone, stretch the taffy away from you, then fold it straight over, and stretch again. Or pull it over a large hook, much like pulling the ends of a damp towel towards the floor. However you do it, be sure to fold taffy end-to-end and pull again and again, until it lightens and has a shiny finish.)

6 Start twisting taffies together, barber-pole fashion. Twist and draw out candy into a rope; cut off twisted sections about 18 inches long.

Working with one section at a time, continue twisting and drawing out rope until strands do not separate and rope is of desired thickness.

7 Cut into 6-inch lengths and curve one end of each piece so it forms a cane shape.

8 Let harden. Then wrap in transparent wrap, if you wish.

Molasses Chips

A taffy-like candy to dissolve slowly in the mouth for full flavor

Makes about 1¾ pounds.

2 cups sugar
¾ cup light corn syrup
¼ cup molasses
1 tablespoon butter or margarine
¾ cup water

1 Combine ingredients in a large saucepan. Cook, stirring constantly, until sugar dissolves. Cover pan for 1 minute to allow the steam to wash down the sugar crystals that cling to side of pan, or wipe down the crystals with a damp cloth.

2 Uncover pan; insert candy thermometer. Cook without stirring until candy thermometer reaches 266° (hard ball stage, where syrup when dropped into very cold water forms a ball in the fingers that is hard enough to hold a shape, yet still plastic).

3 Remove from heat; pour syrup onto two well-buttered jelly-roll pans or a very large platter. Cool candy for about 5 minutes, then fold edges to center.

4 When candy is cool enough to handle, butter hands and pull candy into a rope. Pull rope, folding it back on itself as you pull 25 times. When candy loses its transparent appearance but is still "plastic," knead it like bread dough on a well-buttered surface. Flatten candy, then stretch it from one side into a long ribbon-like strip. Cut the ribbon into 1½-inch pieces.

5 Wrap each piece of candy separately in foil or plastic wrap. Store 2 to 3 weeks in a tightly covered container.

CANDY BASICS:

HOW TO STORE SUGARS AND SYRUPS

Granulated, very fine, and 10X sugars. Store all in a very dry place or in a tightly covered container to keep out moisture and prevent lumping. If granulated sugar should harden into a cake, try these first-aid tricks: Cover it, set in a warm place to dry out, then crush in a blender or roll with a rolling pin. If it turns very hard, it's easiest to make it into a sugar-water syrup to use for sweetening beverages or fruits. At times you may find your supply getting ahead of you, but it's good practice to buy often and only what you can use within two or three weeks.

Brown sugar. It needs moisture, so your refrigerator is a perfect keeper. Or, empty the package into a transparent bag and seal tightly; it will stay soft for many weeks. Some cooks place a slice of bread or a cut piece of apple in the canister, and these, too, help to keep the sugar moist. If it cakes, simply put it in a paper bag, wrap the bag in a damp cloth, and let it stand until soft.

Syrups. Your cupboard shelf is the best storage spot. Wipe the neck of the bottle or jar with a damp cloth after each use, and recap lightly. This lets in just enough air to prevent mold and crystallization. The exceptions are fruit syrups, which usually need chilling. Check the label to make sure.

Maple syrup. Once opened, it should be kept in the refrigerator. If mold appears, no harm done. Just skim it off, and heat the syrup to boiling. Or if it forms a crust on top, heat until the sugar dissolves.

Honey. To preserve its fresh flavor and aroma, keep the jar tightly covered in a dry place, for chilling gives it a cloudy look. If it gets sugary and thick, simply heat honey in its jar in lukewarm water until honey is syrupy.

CRUNCHY BRITTLE

Popcorn-Almond Brittle

There's a mouthful of treats in every bite of this brittle

Makes 1¼ pounds.

6 cups unsalted popcorn
1 cup slivered almonds
½ cup chopped candied red cherries
1½ cups sugar
½ cup light corn syrup
½ cup water
½ teaspoon salt
2 tablespoons butter or margarine
1 teaspoon vanilla

1 Spread popcorn, almonds and cherries in a buttered roasting pan and heat in a 350° oven for about 10 minutes. Turn off oven, open door, leave pan in warm oven.
2 Combine sugar, corn syrup, water and salt in a medium-size heavy saucepan.
3 Cook and stir over low heat until sugar is dissolved. Then cook, without stirring, until temperature reaches 300° on the candy thermometer. (A teaspoon of syrup will form brittle threads when dropped into cold water.)
4 Watch the syrup carefully, and as soon as it reaches 300°, remove it from heat. Quickly stir in butter and vanilla, stirring only until butter melts.
5 Remove popcorn mixture from oven. Pour syrup over and toss. Spread mixture thin on a buttered flat surface. Cool. Break into small pieces. Store in a tightly covered tin.

Peanut Brittle

Toasty and crunchy, and full of peanuts, this candy is hard to beat for popularity

Makes 2¾ pounds.

3 cups sugar
1¼ cups water
½ cup light corn syrup
3 tablespoons butter or margarine
1 pound Spanish peanuts
1 teaspoon baking soda
1 tablespoon water
1½ teaspoons vanilla

(continued)

Who can resist gifts such as **Pralines** and **Butter-Nut Brittle,** with a little fudge and nuts added?

1 Butter 2 large cookie sheets.
2 Combine sugar, water and corn syrup in large heavy saucepan. Bring to boiling over medium heat, stirring constantly.
3 Boil mixture without stirring until candy thermometer registers 270° (soft crack stage). Remove from heat. Add butter or margarine and peanuts.
4 Continue cooking mixture until candy thermometer registers 300°. (A teaspoonful of syrup will separate into brittle threads when dropped in cold water.) Remove from heat. Mix baking soda with the 1 tablespoon water; add to hot candy with vanilla.
5 When bubbles subside, pour candy out onto the prepared cookie sheets as thinly as possible. Cool; break into pieces. Store in air-tight container with wax paper between the layers.

Butternut Brittle

Baking soda makes this candy puffy-light and shattery-crisp. A good keeper, it can be made weeks ahead of the holiday rush

Makes about 2 pounds

2 cups sugar
1 cup light corn syrup
1 cup water
3 cups dry toasted mixed nuts (from 2 about-9-ounce jars)
 OR: 3 cups unsalted roasted mixed nuts
2 tablespoons butter or margarine
2 teaspoons vanilla
2 teaspoons baking soda

1 Butter a baking pan, 15x10x1.
2 Mix sugar, corn syrup, and water in a large *heavy* saucepan; cover; heat to boiling. Uncover and cook rapidly to 236° on a candy thermometer. (A teaspoon of syrup dropped into cold water will form a soft ball.)
3 Stir in nuts slowly, keeping mixture bubbling all the time, then cook rapidly, stirring constantly, to 280° on candy thermometer. (A teaspoon of syrup dropped in cold water will form a very hard ball.)
4 Stir in butter or margarine; continue cooking to 300° on candy thermometer. (A teaspoon of syrup dropped into cold water will separate into threads that are hard and brittle.) Remove from heat.
5 Stir in vanilla; sprinkle soda over top quickly, then stir vigorously about 15 seconds, or until mixture is puffy.
6 Pour into prepared pan at once; cool completely. Break into bite-size pieces. Store in a container that has a tight-fitting lid.

MELT-IN-THE-MOUTH DROPS AND JELLIES

Butterscotch Drops

These melt-in-the-mouth drops stay fresh and chewy for many months and are a sweet reward for all little boys and girls

Makes about 5 dozen (1-inch) candies.

¾ cup sugar
⅔ cup firmly packed light brown sugar
¼ cup light corn syrup
⅔ cup water
6 tablespoons butter or margarine

1 Mix sugar, brown sugar, corn syrup, water and butter in a large heavy saucepan.
2 Cook over medium heat, stirring until sugar is dissolved. Continue cooking, without stirring, to 270° on the candy thermometer. (A teaspoon of syrup will separate into hard but not brittle threads when dropped into cold water.)
3 Remove from heat. Working quickly, drop by half teaspoonfuls onto buttered cookie sheets to form small rounds. When set, wrap in wax

paper to keep candy from sticking together, or place between layers of wax paper in a tightly closed container.

Lemon Drops

These sparkling jewel-like candies owe their special brilliance to the tiny tart pans that mold them

Makes 5 dozen or 1½ pounds.

2 cups sugar
1 cup light corn syrup
½ cup water
½ teaspoon oil of lemon*
2 drops yellow food coloring

1 Coat well 10 toy muffin cup pans (6 cups to a pan) or 60 tiny fancy metal molds with vegetable oil. OR: (You may also drop the mixture by teaspoonfuls onto oiled cookie sheets to make patties.)
2 Combine sugar, corn syrup and water in a medium-size heavy saucepan. Heat quickly to boiling, stirring constantly. Wrap a fork with damp paper towel; wipe sugar crystals from side of pan as mixture cooks.
3 Reduce heat to medium and cook, without stirring, to 300° on a candy thermometer. (A teaspoonful of syrup will separate into threads that are hard and brittle when dropped in cold water.)
4 Remove saucepan from heat and stir in oil of lemon and yellow food coloring until mixture stops bubbling.
5 Pour syrup by spoonfuls into oiled molds. (If syrup becomes too hard, return saucepan to very low heat, just until mixture thins, but not long enough for syrup to darken.) Cool candies in molds at least one hour.
6 To remove candies: Insert the pointed tip of a small paring knife around edge of molds and press to loosen. Store in layers, separated by aluminum foil, in a tight-fitting container.

ORANGE DROPS
Follow above directions for LEMON DROPS, increasing the yellow food coloring to ¼ teaspoon and adding 2 drops red food coloring and substituting ½ teaspoon oil of orange* for the ½ teaspoon oil of lemon.
*Oil of lemon and oil of orange are products that can be purchased in any drug store. You can also substitute 1½ teaspoons lemon extract or orange extract for the oils, if you wish.

Turkish Mint Jelly Candies

An after-dinner treat that goes well with a hot drink

Makes about 1 pound

¾ cup granulated sugar
⅔ cup water
5 tablespoons plus ⅓ cup cornstarch
1⅓ cups 10X (confectioners' powdered) sugar
1 cup water
⅛ teaspoon cream of tartar
¼ teaspoon peppermint oil
   green food coloring

1 Grease a 9x5x3-inch loaf pan. Line with wax paper.
2 Place granulated sugar and ⅔ cup water in a heavy 1½-quart pan. Stir over gentle heat until sugar has dissolved, about 3 to 4 minutes. Attach candy thermometer to pan. Increase heat and bring to boil. Boil, without stirring, for 7 to 10 minutes, until candy thermometer registers 240° or a drop of syrup forms a soft ball when dropped into cold water.
3 Meanwhile, mix 5 tablespoons cornstarch with 1 cup 10X sugar and 1 cup water. Stir until boiling (paste will be clear and thick). When the sugar reaches the desired temperature, quickly stir in cream of tartar and pour all at once into the cornstarch mixture. Stir well until smooth, then simmer for 10 minutes over medium heat, stirring constantly. Remove pan from heat. Flavor with peppermint oil and add a few drops green food coloring. Pour into prepared loaf pan. Leave to set unrefrigerated for 12 hours.
4 For coating the candies, sift ⅓ cup 10X sugar and ⅓ cup cornstarch onto a board. Loosen sides of jelled candy in pan and turn out onto board. Cut into 4 strips lengthwise. Cut each strip into 8 pieces. Coat each piece with sugar and cornstarch mixture. Store in box, sprinkling sugar and cornstarch between each layer. Candy will keep for about 4 weeks in an airtight container.

Gum Drops

Cloud-soft, fruity and delicious, these gum drops are also very easy to make

Makes 1¼ pounds.

1 package (1¾ ounces) powdered fruit pectin
¾ cup water
½ teaspoon baking soda
1 cup sugar
1 cup light corn syrup
2 teaspoons imitation strawberry extract
   Red food coloring
   Sugar

1 Combine fruit pectin, water and baking soda in a medium-size saucepan. (This mixture will foam.)
2 Combine sugar and corn syrup in large saucepan.
3 Place both saucepans over high heat. Cook, stirring alternately, until the foam disappears from the fruit pectin mixture and the sugar mixture boils rapidly, about 5 minutes.
4 Pour fruit pectin mixture into boiling sugar mixture in a thin stream, until all pectin is added. Boil mixture, stirring constantly, 1 minute longer.
5 Remove saucepan from heat. Stir in strawberry extract and a few drops of red food coloring.
6 Immediately pour mixture into an 8x8x2-inch pan. For fancy shapes, spoon mixture into tiny tart or hors d'oeuvres pans. Allow to stand at room temperature (do not refrigerate) 3 hours, or until candy is cool and firm.
7 Cut gum drop mixture into fancy shapes with small cutters or cut into cubes with a knife dipped in warm water. Roll in granulated sugar.

GREEN GUM DROPS
Substitute oil of anise for strawberry extract and green food coloring for red.

YELLOW GUM DROPS
Substitute oil of lemon for strawberry extract and yellow food coloring for red.

RED GUM DROPS
Substitute oil of clove (a drop or two) for strawberry extract.

Coconut Clusters

Each little drop tastes like butterscotch fudge laced with plenty of coconut

Makes about 1½ pounds

1½ cups firmly packed brown sugar
¼ cup granulated sugar
¼ teaspoon ground cinnamon
½ cup water
2 tablespoons butter or margarine
½ teaspoon vanilla
1 can (about 4 ounces) flaked coconut

1 Combine brown and granulated sugars, cinnamon, and water in a medium-size heavy saucepan. Heat slowly, stirring constantly, until sugars dissolve, then cook rapidly, without stirring, to 238° on a candy thermometer. (A teaspoonful of syrup will form a soft ball when dropped in cold water.) Remove from heat at once.

2 Stir in butter or margarine. Cool mixture in pan on a wire rack to 200°. Stir in vanilla and coconut, then beat several minutes, or until mixture holds its shape but is still glossy.

3 Drop by teaspoonfuls, 1 inch apart, on wax paper. Let stand until firm.

TIME-TESTED CANDY TREASURES

Almond Butter Crunch

A munchy candy sandwich, with a buttery crunchy center between two chocolate and nut layers

Makes 1 pound.

  1½ cups (12 ounces) whole blanched almonds, chopped
    1 cups (2 sticks) butter or margarine
  1½ cups sugar
    3 tablespoons light corn syrup
    3 tablespoons water
    1 package (8 ounces) semi-sweet chocolate squares

1 Place chopped almonds on a cookie sheet; toast in moderate oven (375°) 10 minutes, or until lightly golden.

2 Combine butter or margarine, sugar, corn syrup and water in a medium-size heavy saucepan. Cook over medium heat, stirring constantly, to 300° on candy thermometer. (A teaspoonful of syrup will separate into brittle threads when dropped in cold water.) Remove from heat; stir in 1 cup of the toasted almonds. Pour into a buttered 13x9x2-inch pan, spreading quickly and evenly; cool. Turn out onto wax paper.

3 Melt chocolate squares in the top of a double boiler over hot water; remove from heat. Spread half the melted chocolate over top of candy; sprinkle with ¼ cup nuts; let set for about 20 minutes; turn candy over and spread with remaining chocolate and sprinkle with remaining nuts. Let stand until set. Break into pieces.

Chocolate Truffles

Bite-size confections—easy to make and even easier to eat

Makes about 3 dozen.

  1 package (6 ounces) semi-sweet chocolate pieces
  2 tablespoons brandy
  2 tablespoons light corn syrup
  ⅔ cup sifted 10X (confectioners') sugar
  ½ cup finely chopped filberts or almonds
    Chocolate or multi-colored decorating candies

1 Heat chocolate pieces, brandy and corn syrup in top of double boiler over hot water, stirring often, until chocolate is melted. Beat with rotary beater until smooth; remove from heat.

2 Stir in 10X sugar and nuts until well blended; let stand until cool enough to handle (about 5 minutes).

3 Shape mixture into small balls (about 1 teaspoonful each). Roll balls in decorating candies to coat; place in single layer on wax paper in shallow pan; cover loosely until cool. Truffles may also be rolled in sifted unsweetened cocoa just before serving. Store in tightly covered container.

Old-Fashioned Sponge Candy

Crunchy and porous, like a big candy sponge—kids love it

Makes about 1 pound.

  1 cup sugar
  1 cup dark corn syrup
  1 tablespoon white vinegar
  1 tablespoon baking soda

1 Combine sugar, corn syrup and vinegar in a large saucepan. Cook, stirring constantly, until sugar dissolves. Cover pan for 1 minute to allow the steam to wash down the sugar crystals that cling to side of pan, or wipe down the crystals with a damp cloth.

2 Uncover pan; insert candy thermometer. Cook without stirring until candy thermometer reaches 300° (hard crack stage, when syrup dropped in very cold water separates into hard and brittle threads).

3 Remove from heat; stir in baking soda. Pour
(continued)

into a buttered 9x9x2-inch pan. (It's not necessary to spread, as the mixture will bubble and spread itself); cool in pan on wire rack. Break cooled sponge into pieces. Store 2 to 3 weeks in a tightly covered container with foil or plastic wrap between layers.

Pink Peppermint Patties

These shiny pink and white mint patties are easy to make and fun to decorate

Makes about 5 dozen.

1 package (1 pound) 10X (confectioners') sugar
3 tablespoons light corn syrup
3 tablespoons water
½ teaspoon peppermint extract
    Red food coloring
    ROYAL FROSTING (see index for recipe)

1 Combine 10X sugar, corn syrup and water in the top of a double boiler. Heat over simmering water (do not allow water to boil or steam will dull the tops of the shiny patties), stirring several times, until sugar dissolves and mixture is smooth.
2 Remove from heat, but let mixture stand over hot water to keep soft for shaping. Stir in peppermint extract.
3 To make white candies, drop half of mixture, a teaspoonful at a time, onto cookie sheets to form 1-inch rounds. Let stand until firm.
4 To tint candies, stir a few drops of red food coloring into remaining mixture in top of double boiler, then shape, following directions in Step 3. Let stand until firm.
5 Decorate each with a dainty leaf or flower design, using ROYAL FROSTING.

Butterscotch Patties

Little wafers of golden butterscotch to let melt slowly in your mouth

Makes 8 dozen 1-inch patties.

2 cups sugar
¾ cup dark corn syrup

¼ cup water
¼ cup milk
⅓ cup butter or margarine

1 Lightly butter 3 large cookie sheets.
2 Combine sugar, corn syrup, water and milk in a medium-size heavy saucepan. Bring to boiling over medium heat, stirring constantly. Cook, stirring often, to 260° on a candy thermometer; add butter or margarine.
3 Cook, stirring constantly, to 280° on a candy thermometer. (A teaspoonful of syrup will separate into threads that are hard but not brittle when dropped in cold water.) Remove from heat.
4 Drop hot syrup from tip of teaspoon onto cookie sheets to form 1-inch patties; or pour into a 9x9x2-inch pan, and, when almost set, mark into small squares. When firm, turn out and break apart.

Basic Marshmallows

Once you have this basic recipe down, you can vary the ingredients for your own marshmallows

Makes about 1½ pounds

2 cups sifted sugar
¾ cup hot water
1 cup light corn syrup
1½ teaspoons vanilla or other flavoring
2½ tablespoons unflavored gelatin softened in ¾ cup cold water

1 In large pan, combine sugar, hot water, ½ cup syrup. Blend well; cook over high heat until candy thermometer reads 240°.
2 Turn off heat, add ½ cup corn syrup. Add softened gelatin to syrup. Stir gently.
3 Pour at once into an 8″ ovenproof glass bowl. Immediately begin beating it, accelerating speed. Beat hard for 10 minutes, or until mixture is lukewarm, snowy white, and heavy.
4 Add flavoring.
5 Pour into 7″ pans greased with vegetable shortening. Store 8 hours. Cover with 10X (confectioners' powdered) sugar, and cut with greased knife. Roll pieces in 10X sugar to cover well.

Candies are for everyone. And here is a lineup of hard and soft candies—the kind that melt-in-your-mouth and the chewy kind—that you can make yourself. The commercial kind can't rival them.

Cherry Puffs

Tinted coconut and candied fruit top each of these wispy sweet morsels

Makes about 1¼ pounds

1 cup flaked coconut
  Red and green food colorings
2 cups sugar
½ cup light corn syrup
½ cup water
2 egg whites
1 teaspoon vanilla
  Candied red cherries, halved
  Candied green cherries, halved

1 Place ½ cup of the coconut, a drop or two red food coloring, and a drop or two water in a jar with a tight-fitting lid; shake until coconut is evenly tinted. Repeat with remaining coconut and green food coloring. Set aside for Step 5.

2 Combine sugar, corn syrup, and water in a medium-size heavy saucepan; heat, stirring constantly, to boiling. (Have a fork wrapped in a piece of damp cheesecloth handy and wipe off any sugar crystals that form on side of pan as mixture heats.)

3 Cook rapidly, without stirring, to 260° on a candy thermometer. (A teaspoonful of syrup will form a hard ball when dropped in cold water.) Remove pan from heat.

4 While syrup cooks, beat egg whites until they stand in firm peaks in a medium-size bowl. *Beating constantly,* pour in syrup in a fine stream; beat in vanilla, then continue beating until mixture is very stiff and holds its shape. Stir in a few drops red food coloring to tint pale pink. (continued)

5 Drop mixture by teaspoonfuls into small mounds onto foil- or wax-paper-lined cooky sheets. Top half with pink coconut and red candied cherries, and remaining with green coconut and green cherries. Let candies stand until firm.

CANDY BASICS:
TOPPERS AND TRIMS

Cakes, pies, cookies, candies, puddings, and ice-cream desserts take on a professional look with a garnish of grated chocolate or chocolate curls. To grate: Start with cold chocolate, a dry cold grater, and cold hands. Rub the square up and down over the grating surface, working quickly and handling the chocolate as little as possible.

To make curls: Warm a square of chocolate slightly at room temperature, then, for little curls, shave thin strips from the narrow side with a vegetable parer; for large ones, from the bottom. Pick up the curls with a wooden pick (otherwise they shatter) and chill until firm before arranging on food.

NO-COOK CANDIES

Stuffed Dates

With pineapple and brown sugar in filling, an inspired sweet

Makes about 1½ pounds

1 can (8¼ ounces) crushed pineapple
1 cup oven-toasted rice cereal, crushed
2 tablespoons brown sugar
1 teaspoon grated orange rind
1 package (8 ounces) pitted dates
   Granulated sugar

1 Drain syrup from pineapple. (Save to add to a fruit cup.) Blend pineapple, cereal, brown sugar, and orange rind in a small bowl.
2 Make a slit in side of each date; spread slits slightly to open; fill each with a rounded teaspoonful pineapple mixture. Roll in granulated sugar on wax paper to coat well. Store in a tightly covered container.

Apricot Creams

Dried fruits make the nicest bite-size sweets—like little no-cook candies

Makes about 1½ pounds

½ cup golden raisins
½ cup toasted slivered almonds
1 cup 10X (confectioners' powdered) sugar
2 tablespoons dairy sour cream
1 package (11 ounces) dried apricot halves

1 Chop raisins and almonds; blend with 10X sugar and sour cream in a small bowl.
2 Separate apricot halves; spoon a scant teaspoonful raisin mixture in center of each half. Chill.

Gumdrop Whimsies

BASIC DIRECTIONS
Spread about ¼ cup granulated sugar at a time onto a pastry board. With a rolling pin, roll out medium-size gumdrops in sugar, turning several times to keep them from sticking, then shape, following directions below. Let candies stand on a wire rack until slightly dry and firm enough to hold shape.

CALICO ROLLS
To make each, roll out 1 gumdrop to a 2-inch round. Cut about 6 small pieces from different-color gumdrops and arrange in a round layer; place rolled-out gumdrop on top. Roll all again into a bigger flat round, then roll up, jelly-roll fashion.

RAINBOW TRIANGLES
To make each, roll out 2 each red, yellow, and green gumdrops to a 2-inch round. Brush each round lightly with a pastry brush dipped in water; stack rounds, alternating colors. Let stand several hours to dry, then cut in quarters.

WHIRLIGIGS
To make each, roll out 2 contrasting-color gumdrops to 3-inch rounds. Place one on top of the other; fold in half, then roll into a cone shape.

ROSES
To make each, roll out a gumdrop to a 3-inch round; cut in half. Roll up one half, crimping cut edge tightly with finger to make base of flower and flaring out top edge into petals. Roll remaining half around first half the same way, pressing together tightly at base and shaping

into petals to make a full, open rose. Roll out a green gumdrop to a 2-inch round, cut out leaf shapes; press onto base of rose. Place, base down, on a wire rack to dry. Snip two small strips from a contrasting-color gumdrop and tuck into center of rose.

Note: To store, layer with wax paper or transparent wrap between in a shallow pan; cover; store in a cool place.

Quick-as-a-Wink Fudge

Prepare 1 package fudge frosting mix, following label directions for fudge; stir in ½ cup chopped walnuts. Spread evenly in a buttered 8-inch foil pie plate or in a wax-paper-lined pan, 8x8x2. Sprinkle ¼ cup chopped walnuts over. Makes about three dozen pieces.

Fondant Bonbons

Young cooks will be tickled to help shape and trim these no-cook fancies

Makes about 1½ pounds

    4 tablespoons (½ stick) butter or margarine
    ¼ cup light corn syrup
    ⅛ teaspoon salt
    3½ cups sifted 10X (confectioners' powdered) sugar

1 Cream butter or margarine until soft in a medium-size bowl; stir in corn syrup and salt, then 10X sugar until completely blended. Knead a few minutes, or until smooth.
2 Divide mixture into four bowls; flavor, shape, and decorate, following directions below.

Sunshine Meltaways

Add ¼ teaspoon lemon extract and a drop or two yellow food coloring to fondant in one bowl; knead in until completely blended. Divide into 24 even pieces; flatten each to a 1½-inch thin round on a cooky sheet. Decorate with red cinnamon-candy hearts or semisweet-chocolate pieces. Chill until firm.

Snowdrops

Add ¼ teaspoon vanilla to fondant in one bowl; knead in until completely blended. Divide into 24 even pieces; flatten each to a 1½-inch thin round on a cooky sheet. Decorate with red cinnamon-candy hearts, slivered red or green candied cherries, walnuts or pecans, or colored decorating sugars of your choice. Chill until firm.

Chocolate Creams

Add 1 tablespoon dry cocoa powder (*not a mix*) and ¼ teaspoon vanilla to fondant in one bowl; knead in until completely blended. Divide into 24 even pieces; flatten each to a 1½-inch thin round on a cooky sheet. Decorate with chocolate sprinkles or colored decorating sugars of your choice. Chill until firm.

Orange Patties

Add ¼ teaspoon orange extract and a drop each red and yellow food colorings to fondant in one bowl; knead in until completely blended. Divide into 24 even pieces; flatten each to a 1½-inch thin round on a cooky sheet. Decorate with chocolate sprinkles or colored decorating sugars of your choice. Chill until firm.

Choco-Almond Triangles

Semisweet chocolate "frosts" a rich coconut-almond layer for these sweet-tooth tempters

Makes 72 triangles

    1½ cups toasted slivered almonds (from two 5-ounce cans)
    1 can (about 4 ounces) flaked coconut
    2 tablespoons butter or margarine, melted
    1 package (1 pound) sifted 10X (confectioners' powdered) sugar
    ⅓ cup evaporated milk
    3 squares semisweet chocolate

1 Chop 1 cup of the almonds. (Set remaining ½ cup aside for decorating triangles in Step 4.)
2 Combine chopped almonds with coconut and melted butter or margarine in a medium-size bowl; blend in 10X sugar, alternately with evaporated milk, until well-mixed. Spoon into a but-

(continued)

tered pan, 9x9x2, pressing down firmly with back of spoon to make an even layer.

3 Melt semisweet chocolate in a small bowl over simmering water; spread over coconut layer. Chill at least 30 minutes, or until chocolate is firm.

4 Cut lengthwise, then crosswise into sixths to make 36 squares; remove from pan. Cut each square in half diagonally. Gently press a slivered almond in top of each. Chill again.

Note: To store, place in a single layer in a shallow pan; cover with transparent wrap or foil and keep chilled so chocolate will stay firm.

Marshmallow Popcorn Balls

They're as easy as melting marshmallows and popping corn. Youngsters will be tickled to help with the shaping

Makes 16

32 large marshmallows (from an about-10-ounce package)
4 tablespoons (½ stick) butter or margarine
    Green food coloring
4 cups unsalted freshly popped popcorn

1 Combine marshmallows and butter or margarine in the top of a double boiler; heat, stirring often, over simmering water 15 minutes, or until marshmallows melt. Stir in a few drops food coloring to tint light green.

2 Pour over popcorn in a large bowl; toss with a wooden spoon until evenly coated.

3 Divide into 16 even mounds on wax paper. Butter hands lightly and shape into balls.

4 Trim with slivered red candied cherries and silver candies, if you wish. Place on wire racks until firm.

Note: To store, layer with wax paper or transparent wrap between in a shallow pan; cover.

Butterscotch Nougats

They taste so creamy smooth and rich with a now-and-then bite of cherries and nuts

Makes about 2 pounds

1 package (6 ounces) butterscotch-flavor pieces
1 small can evaporated milk (⅔ cup)
2½ cups sifted 10X (confectioners' powdered) sugar
½ cup chopped pistachio nuts

¼ cup red candied cherries (from a 4-ounce jar), chopped
1 can (about 4 ounces) flaked coconut

1 Combine butterscotch-flavor pieces and evaporated milk in a medium-size saucepan; heat, stirring constantly, just until butterscotch pieces melt.

2 Stir in 10X sugar, nuts, and cherries. Chill about an hour, or until firm enough to handle.

3 Shape, a rounded teaspoonful at a time, into small balls; roll in coconut on wax paper. Chill several hours, or until firm.

Note: To store, layer candies with wax paper or transparent wrap between in a tightly covered container. Keep in a cool place.

Almond Truffles

Make a large batch—the family will keep on enjoying them

Makes about 40

6 squares (1 ounce each) semi-sweet chocolate
2 tablespoons light cream
6 ounces (⅔ cup) almond paste* or marzipan
¼ teaspoon almond extract
    for decoration: chocolate or cocoa powder; flaked coconut; chopped almonds; chocolate or multicolored sprinkles

1 Melt chocolate in top of double boiler (or in mixing bowl) over hot, not boiling, water. When completely melted, remove from heat and stir in cream, marzipan or almond paste, and almond extract. Stir until well mixed. Set 3 tablespoons of each decoration on wax paper.

2 Make small balls of candy by rolling the mixture between palms of your hands, using a heaping half-teaspoon for each ball. Roll at once in decorations.

3 Refrigerate truffles until firm, about 2 hours. Store in cool place or in refrigerator.

*Note: As an alternative, grind 1 cup blanched almonds as fine as possible in electric blender. Add to melted chocolate with additional 1 tablespoon of light cream and 1 cup 10X confectioners' sugar.

Marzipan Vegetable Bouquet

Young hands are good at forming these shapes

Makes about 2 pounds

2 cans (8 ounces each) almond paste
1 jar (about 7 ounces) marshmallow cream
¼ cup light corn syrup
3¾ cups sifted 10X (confectioners' powdered) sugar
Yellow, red, green, and blue food colorings

1 Crumble almond paste into a medium-size bowl; blend in marshmallow cream and corn syrup. Stir in enough of the 10X sugar to make a very stiff dough.
2 Sprinkle remaining 10X sugar on a pastry board; turn out almond mixture into sugar. Knead 5 to 6 minutes, or until smooth and sugar is worked in completely.
3 Pinch off mixture, about a half teaspoonful at a time, and shape between palms of hands into carrots, peas in pods, radishes, yellow squash, eggplant, and potatoes, or other vegetables of your choice. Let stand on wax paper for several hours, or until dry.
4 When ready to decorate, mix small amounts of food colorings with equal parts of water in custard cups. Brush lightly over "vegetables" to tint. Let stand again until dry. Store in refrigerator.

Fudge Ribbons

Candylike butterscotch and chocolate pieces are your ready-to-go secrets

Makes about 1 pound

1 package (6 ounces) butterscotch-flavor pieces
⅔ cup sweetened condensed milk (from a 14- or 15-ounce can)
2 teaspoons vanilla
1 package (6 ounces) semisweet-chocolate pieces
1 teaspoon instant coffee

1 Melt butterscotch-flavor pieces in the top of a double boiler over simmering water; remove from heat.
2 Stir in ⅓ cup of the sweetened condensed milk (not evaporated) and 1 teaspoon of the vanilla. Spread evenly into a well-buttered pan, 9x9x2, to make a thin layer.
3 Wash double-boiler top and melt semisweet-chocolate pieces the same way; remove from heat. Stir in remaining ⅓ cup sweetened condensed milk, 1 teaspoon vanilla, and instant coffee. Spread evenly into a second well-buttered pan, 9x9x2. Chill layers several hours, or until firm.
4 Cut each into 6 strips, 1½ inches wide; stack three each butterscotch and chocolate strips, alternately, to make 2 six-layer bars; wrap each tightly in foil. Chill several hours, or overnight.
5 Cut each bar into 24 thin slices with a sharp knife.
Note: To store, keep bars wrapped and chilled, ready to slice just before serving.

CANDY BASICS:

HOW TO PACK CANDIES FOR MAILING

Choose varieties that travel well—fudge, caramels, or fruit drops. Use a metal container and place a layer of crushed wax paper in bottom, then cut dividers of cardboard and fit into the box to help keep the pieces from shifting about.

After arranging candies attractively in their gift box, add lid and tape or tie shut for extra protection. Set container in a strong, larger carton and fill in the spaces with unsalted popped corn or crushed paper to cushion the bounce.

Wrap outer carton in heavy brown paper, tie securely, affix label (printed or typed) on one side only, and mark the package "Keep from heat." Plan to mail gifts by December 1, and remember to include ZIP Code for speedier delivery.

Holiday Cookies and Candies

There are many ways to enjoy the traditional holiday season, and one of the best of them is baking cookies and candies. Many of these you'll save for the family; but guests who drop in will be delighted by the gleeful sight of a saucer or two of brightly-colored jewels. Also, let absent family and friends in on your festivities. Mail them a batch of your favorite cookies or candies.

Dreamland Cut-outs

Finnish children call these thin crisp spicy ginger cookies piparkakut.

Bake at 350° for 7 minutes.
Makes 1½ dozen
large and 6 dozen tiny cut-outs,
plus 5 dozen round cookies

¾ cup molasses
1 teaspoon grated orange rind
1 teaspoon ground cinnamon
1 teaspoon ground ginger
⅛ teaspoon ground cloves
4 cups sifted all-purpose flour
1 teaspoon baking soda
¼ teaspoon salt
½ cup (1 stick) butter or margarine
¼ cup sugar
1 egg
    ORNAMENTAL FROSTING (recipe follows)

1 Combine molasses, orange rind, cinnamon, ginger, and cloves in a small saucepan; heat, stirring constantly, just to boiling; cool.
2 Measure flour, soda, and salt into sifter.
3 Cream butter or margarine with sugar until fluffy in a large bowl; beat in egg and cooled molasses mixture.
4 Sift in dry ingredients, a third at a time, blending well to make a stiff dough. Chill several hours, overnight, or until firm enough to roll.
5 Divide dough in half; wrap one half in wax

Good on the eye and exciting to the taste, these Christmas cookies could just as easily be any-season cookies. Set your. mind to creating cookies that reflect a particular season or some hobby of the family.

paper, foil, or transparent wrap and chill for making round cookies in Step 7. Divide remaining dough into quarters, for it's easier to roll a small amount at a time. Return three quarters to refrigerator.
6 Roll out dough *very thin* on a lightly floured pastry cloth or board. Cut out fancy cookies using homemade cardboard pattern or your favorite cookie cutters, floured. Transfer with spatula to ungreased cookie sheets. Roll and cut out remaining three quarters of chilled dough this same way.
7 Use wrapped half of dough for round cookies, using an about-2-inch cutter.
8 Bake all in moderate oven (350°) 7 minutes, or until firm. Remove from cookie sheets; cool completely on wire racks.
9 Decorate with plain or tinted ORNAMENTAL FROSTING. Leave round cookies plain, or frost, as you wish.

Ornamental Frosting

Store any leftover frosting in a covered jar in the refrigerator for another day's baking.

Makes about ¾ cup

1 egg white
⅛ teaspoon cream of tartar
⅛ teaspoon vanilla
1¾ cups sifted 10X (confectioners' powdered) sugar

1 Beat egg white, cream of tartar, and vanilla until foamy in a small bowl. Beat in 10X sugar gradually until frosting stands in firm peaks and is stiff enough to hold a sharp line when cut through with a knife.
2 Use plain or divide into custard cups and tint with food colorings, if you wish.

Snowcap Cookie Cottage

Build this little cottage of chocolate-walnut cookie dough to admire first, then eat within two or three days

Bake at 375° for 20 minutes.
Makes 1 cookie house

3½ cups sifted all-purpose flour
1½ teaspoons baking soda
 1 teaspoon salt
 ¾ cup (1½ sticks) butter or margarine
 ¾ cup vegetable shortening
 1 cup granulated sugar
 1 cup firmly packed brown sugar
 3 eggs
 1 teaspoon vanilla
 3 packages (6 ounces each) semisweet-chocolate pieces
1½ cups chopped walnuts (from an 8-ounce can)
   FLUFFY FROSTING *(recipe follows)*
   Green decorating sugar
   Silver and red candies
   Birthday-cake candles

1 Grease a baking pan, 15x10x1; line with wax paper; grease paper.
2 Measure flour, soda, and salt into sifter.
3 Cream butter or margarine and shortening with granulated and brown sugars until fluffy in a large bowl; beat in eggs and vanilla. Sift in dry ingredients, a third at a time, blending well to make a soft dough. Stir in semisweet-chocolate pieces and nuts.
4 Measure out 3 cups of dough and spread in prepared pan. (Set remaining dough aside for a second baking.)
5 Bake in moderate oven (375°) 20 minutes, or until top springs back when lightly pressed with fingertip. Cool in pan on wire rack 5 minutes; loosen around edge with knife; invert onto wire rack; peel off wax paper; cool layer completely.
6 Wash, dry, and prepare pan as in Step 1; spread remaining dough in pan; bake and cool as in Step 5.
7 Make house: Cover a piece of heavy cardboard, 8x6 inches, with foil for base of house.
8 Cut one cookie layer, following Diagram A,

(continued)

Any young cook will enjoy helping to make this **Snowcap Cookie Cottage** and the cut-out cookies.

into 2 pieces, each 9x4 inches, for roof; 1 piece, 6x7 inches, for one end; and 2 squares, each 1½ inches, for front and back of chimney.

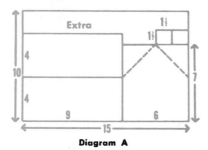

Diagram A

9 Cut second cookie layer, following Diagram B, into 2 pieces, each 8x4 inches, for side walls; 1 piece, 6x7 inches, for other end; and 2 pieces, each 1¾x2 inches, for sides of chimney. Trim the two 6x7-inch pieces as marked with dotted lines in diagrams to make slanted roof. Cut a wedge-shape piece 1 inch deep out of bottom of the two side chimney pieces so chimney will fit over roof. Cut 2 windows and a door in front wall, 2 windows in back, and 2 in each of the end walls.

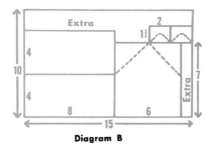

Diagram B

10 Make FLUFFY FROSTING. Spread part on side edges of front and back walls. Stand upright on cardboard base and hold in place, pressing on end walls firmly, and adding more frosting, if needed, to form shell of house. Hold in place a few minutes, then let stand 15 minutes to dry.
11 Spread top edge of front wall and slanted edges of end walls with frosting; set half of roof in place; hold a few minutes, then let stand 5 minutes. Set other section of roof in place the same way. Let house stand 15 minutes to dry completely.
12 Put chimney together with frosting, keeping straight edges even. Let stand, top down, 15 minutes, then set in place on roof.
13 When ready to decorate outside of house, beat 1 to 2 teaspoons water into remaining frosting to soften enough to give a drifted-snow effect. Spoon into a cake-decorating set. Using

writing tip, pipe ribbons across roof to resemble shingles. Change to large round tip and press out frosting generously around chimney, door, windows, corners of house, and edges of roof, letting some drip down for "icicles." Trim door with a frosting "tree;" sprinkle with green sugar; outline with silver candies and place a red candy on top. Stand candles in windows.

FLUFFY FROSTING
Beat 3 egg whites with ¼ teaspoon cream of tartar and 1 teaspoon vanilla until foamy-white and double in volume in a large bowl. Beat in 6 cups (about 1½ packages) sifted 10X (confectioners' powdered) sugar very slowly until frosting stands in soft peaks and holds a line when cut through with a knife.

A GINGERBREAD CHURCH CHILDREN CAN HELP BUILD

From the oven comes a most enchanting Christmas scene—a gingerbread church, horse and carriage and evergreen trees. With a candle inside, shafts of light stream through the sugar-crystal stained windows.

Gingerbread Dough

Bake at 300° for 20 minutes.
Makes 1 church,
1 sleigh, 2 horses,
2 large trees and 2 small trees

5½ cups sifted all-purpose flour
1 teaspoon baking soda
1 teaspoon salt
3 teaspoons ground cinnamon
2 teaspoons ground ginger
2 teaspoons ground cloves
1 teaspoon ground nutmeg
1 cup vegetable shortening
1 cup sugar
1 cup molasses
1 egg

1 Sift flour, baking soda, salt, cinnamon, ginger, cloves, and nutmeg onto wax paper.
2 Beat shortening with sugar until fluffy-light in a large bowl. Beat in molasses and egg. Stir in flour mixture to make a stiff dough. Chill several hours or overnight, until firm enough to roll.
3 Line a cookie sheet with aluminum foil; sprinkle lightly with flour. Roll out ¼ of the

Once you have the fundamentals down, any cooking is easy. This **Gingerbread Church** with rock candy rose windows and white frosting trim looks difficult. But it's easily made with **Gingerbread Dough.**

dough to a ⅛-inch thickness on foil. (This should cover the entire cookie sheet.)

4 Arrange as many pattern pieces as possible on dough, allowing at least ½ inch between pieces; cut out pieces with a sharp knife. Carefully lift away all dough trims and save for rerolls.

5 Bake in very slow oven (300°) 20 minutes, or until cookies feel firm to the touch. Remove cookie sheet from oven and trim any cookie edges that are not straight while cookies are still warm. Cool cookies on cookie sheet on a wire rack for 5 minutes, then slide off foil and cool completely.

Note: If cookie pieces should break while assembling, simply put together with "cement" and cover with ROYAL FROSTING as part of the decoration.

Royal Frosting

Makes enough to decorate church, sleigh, horses, 2 large trees and 2 small trees

    2 egg whites
    1 teaspoon lemon juice
3½ cups sifted 10X (confectioners' powdered) sugar
    Blue, green, and yellow food coloring

Beat egg whites and lemon juice until foamy in a medium-size bowl. Slowly beat in sugar, until frosting stands in firm peaks and is stiff enough to hold a sharp line when cut through with a knife. Divide half the frosting among 3 small bowls. Tint one blue, one green, and one

(continued)

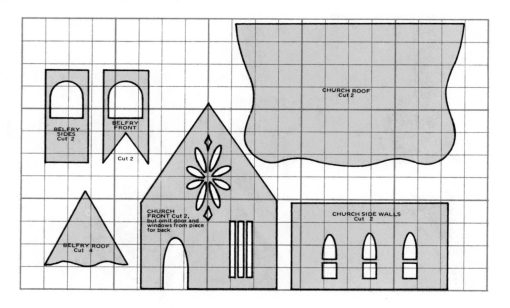

HOW TO ENLARGE PATTERNS

Draw crisscross lines, vertically and horizontally, with a ruler, spacing the lines as indicated. Then copy our pattern, one square at a time, using a ruler or compass if necessary. Cut out enlarged pattern and use as directed.

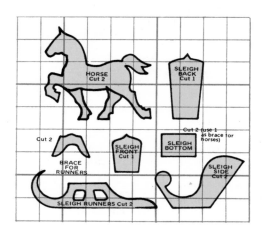

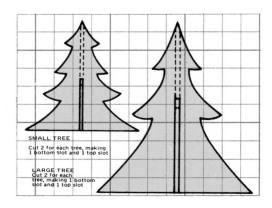

yellow with food colorings. Leave remaining half of frosting white. Keep all frostings covered with damp paper toweling to keep from drying until ready to use.

Sugar "Cement"

Spread 1 cup sugar in a small heavy skillet; heat slowly until sugar melts and starts to turn pale golden in color. Use immediately.

Church with Rose Window

GINGERBREAD DOUGH
Rock candy crystals
Red food coloring
Sugar "Cement"
Royal Frosting

1 Cut out GINGERBREAD DOUGH, following pattern directions for church. Press pieces of rock candy into dough to form the "stained glass" effect; brush red food coloring on rock candy to tint.
2 Bake and cool, following cookie dough directions.
3 To assemble: Dip the edge of cookie pieces into "cement," then quickly press together, following diagram.
4 Fit a pastry bag with a small star tip; fill bag and decorate with ROYAL FROSTING.

Christmas Trees

GINGERBREAD DOUGH
ROYAL FROSTING

1 Cut out GINGERBREAD DOUGH, following pattern directions for large and small trees. Bake and cool, following cookie dough directions.
2 As soon as cookies come out of oven, trim cut-out slots if they have filled in while baking.
3 Fit trees together.
4 Decorate with ROYAL FROSTING.

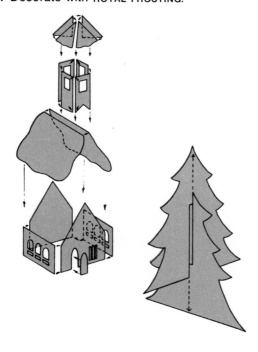

Sleigh and Horses

GINGERBREAD DOUGH
ROYAL FROSTING

1 Cut out GINGERBREAD DOUGH, following pattern directions for sleigh and horses.
2 Bake, following cookie dough directions. As soon as cookies come out of the oven, remove sleigh front and lay over the side of a small jar to give the curve for sleigh front.
3 To assemble: Dip the edge of cookie pieces into "cement" and press together, following assembly diagram for sleigh.
4 Dip second sleigh bottom into "cement" and press together, following assembly directions.
5 Decorate with ROYAL FROSTING.

Peppermint Shrubs

Teenagers can easily make these

Makes 1 dozen small shrubs

⅔ *cup sugar*
⅔ *cup light corn syrup*
½ *teaspoon salt*
½ *teaspoon peppermint extract*
  Green food coloring
4 *cups puffed-rice cereal*

1 Combine sugar, corn syrup, salt, and peppermint extract in a large saucepan; tint a delicate green with food coloring. Heat slowly, stirring constantly, just until sugar dissolves. Remove from heat.
2 Stir in cereal; toss with a wooden spoon until evenly coated. Cook, stirring constantly, over medium heat 5 minutes, or until mixture is very sticky.
3 Turn out onto a large sheet of wax paper or foil; let stand a few minutes to cool. (Cereal stays sticky enough to mold even when cool.)
4 Press into small rounds or pyramids to resemble shrubs or bushes. Set on wax paper or foil to dry.
5 Leave plain or, for a snowy look, brush very lightly with light corn syrup and sprinkle with grated coconut.

Prune Clusters

Little cooks can make these chocolate fruit-and-nut candies once the chopping's done—they're that easy

Makes 3 dozen

1 cup (6-ounce package) semisweet-chocolate pieces
1 cup finely cut pitted dried prunes (from a 12-ounce package)
½ cup coarsely chopped salted peanuts
½ cup flaked coconut
½ cup finely chopped salted peanuts

1 Melt semisweet-chocolate pieces in top of double boiler over hot water. Remove from heat; stir in prunes and coarsely chopped peanuts until fruit and nuts are well-coated.
2 Sprinkle coconut and finely chopped peanuts on separate sheets of wax paper or foil. Drop half of prune mixture, a teaspoonful at a time, onto coconut; roll into balls. Place in single layer on cookie sheet. Repeat with remaining prune mixture, rolling in peanuts. Chill all until firm.

Sparkles

To go along with any type of party

Makes about 1½ pounds candy

1 package (about 11 ounces) mixed dried fruits
1 jar (8 ounces) mixed candied fruits
1 can flaked coconut

2 tablespoons lemon juice
Sugar
Small red and green gumdrops

1 Put dried and candied fruits through food chopper, using fine blade; add coconut and lemon juice; mix well.
2 Form into small patties; dust with sugar and decorate with a red or green gumdrop. OR: Shape into 1½-inch-long rolls; dust with sugar and add a cut red gumdrop "flame."

Choco-Banana Pops

Youngsters will raid the ice-box to get at these jewels

Makes 1 dozen

1 package (6 ounces) semisweet-chocolate pieces
6 firm ripe bananas
12 long wooden skewers

1 Melt semisweet-chocolate pieces in top of double boiler over simmering water; remove from heat but keep hot over hot water.
2 Peel bananas; cut in half crosswise; insert a skewer into each.
3 Frost each half with melted chocolate, holding by its skewer handle; place in a single layer in a chilled buttered shallow pan.
4 Freeze 2 to 3 hours, or until firm. Slip a fluted paper baking cup or a paper napkin onto handle of each "lollipop" before serving.

INDEX